From Bushman to Bush

As History Has Brought Us to a Point of No Return

Farhoud Rastegar

Strategic Book Group

Strategic Book Group
P.O. Box 333
Durham CT 06422
www.StrategicBookClub.com

ISBN: 978-1-60976-519-4

Typography and page composition by J. K. Eckert & Company, Inc.

Dedicated to all my teachers, including my grandma, my parents, and my wife, Mitra. I want to thank all the living beings whose love and companionship has taught me so much and from whom I have been given such great opportunities to learn.

Contents

Introduction

IMMIGRANTS OF AMERICA

Shortly after I was eighteen years old, I found the opportunity to move to San Diego, USA. It had been a growing dream of mine, ever since I was five years old, to someday become an American. My awareness began as I recognize I had to look for something else rather than my immediate environment, something that would be closer to the truth. As I grew older, and started socializing with the people in the society of Iran, I realized the dogma and the culture my surrounding was offering or dictating me to have was not what I had been looking for. I was in search of the truth, the purpose and the meaning of life, and I was not finding it anywhere in my surroundings.

I had formed a different life for myself at home. I would be watching the TV series the "Wild, Wild West," "I Dream of Jeannie," "Bewitched," "Key Serra Serra," "Gilligan's Island," "Mission Impossible," and "Star Trek" among so many other American TV series, and I would structure my own world. I fell in love with the culture my TV world was representing and bringing to me. The more I watched, the more I got curious to find out what the American culture and ideologies were about. By the time I was sixteen, and as I learned much about the history and culture of America, I had the desire and wish to live nowhere else but America. Ironically, right at this time Iranian people had gone through a series of riots, had thrown shah of Iran—a westernized visionary leader—out of Iran, and had placed an Islamic fanatic gang of anti-American mullahs in charge. Shortly after, the Iran's new regime was broadcasting anti American slogans with all their efforts and all the media they could get their hands on. The punishment for anyone having anything to do with America would have been very severe penalty from lashing to death.

This was a very dangerous time to show any interest towards America and American philosophy and culture. Iranians' intentions were not of anything good towards America and anyone who would incline or sympathize towards America. Never the less, one of my best friends at the time and I decided to conduct our lives as if there were nothing going on around us that could taint our imaginary life within our own bubble. We found this behavior a tool that helped us stay clean of the infection that was taking over the Iranian people's minds. That bubble became our own haven where we had a clear vision of what the Iranian government was putting people through. That clarity gave me the courage to keep my eyes open and see the changes people of Iran were going through. Changes took place rapidly as the blind folded people were unaware of the future result of this intense alter.

The more I saw, the more I realized I would have a battle to fight ahead of me; the fight against the slavery under ignorance and fanatic dogmas in Iran and around the world. As time passed after this chaos, additional number of people joined the anti American slogans of the new Iranian government each day. I felt much trapped and I knew I had to get out. Slowly but surely, the circumstances were getting more dangerous for me to continue living in Iran. Never the less, despite the opportunities I found to live in Germany or England, I resisted against my parents' wish to migrate to those countries. However, eventually with the financial help of my parents' life saving, I decided to move to California the very first chance I got.

There were many obstacles on the way to exit Iran. Iran was going through a war with Iraq at the time, and the government did not want to lose any potential soldiers to send to the front line of that none sense and bloody war. It took a lot of effort and many attempts to finally gather the necessary paper work to exit Iran.

Travel to America

When I finally made it out of Iran, my father accompanied me to make sure I would be well taken care of and be settled in my new environment in America. I remember once we got to America, we were mentally and physically so tired that we picked the very first place the taxi cab driver took us to. We spent that first night in a very shabby and run down hotel in unsafe down town San Diego of 1984.

My father had a hard time relaxing that night. He was very worried about our safety and thought we would be mugged and robbed while we were sleeping in that hotel room. He was restless walking around the small dirty room, as I was at the widow looking outside. I was looking over the dirty ally behind the hotel building and into the city lights that were just shining through in between a few buildings which were blocking the view. And then I took a deep breath after a happy sigh. I was finally home.

Soon after our arrival, my father returned back to Iran, and I was left to live life as it would come to me. As time went on, I learned further more about life, American Ideology, politics and science. And as I continued watching the people around me—in my new surroundings that I had always known as home—I realized that there was a growing sensation of self-sabotage and blame within the people of America. This sensation reached its maximum level when the terror of 9/11 changed our lives as a whole. I realized many people, in a tacit way, felt deep down inside they had something to do with the cause of why the Islamic terrorists attacked America on our own soil. I was watching again, and I felt the pain and its depth that was causing division and doubt within us. I knew right away that I had to say and do something. I had to make people aware of the danger that was coming their way. That is when I started writing a series of weekly chronicles addressing different matters to my patients at my practice. I wrote one issue per week starting September 11, 2006 sharing with others the information I had come across. I knew time was of essence, and did not hesitate to communicate what I had to say to them. After all, I have always disliked being politically correct! Because then I would have to hide the truth, and that is not what I grew up looking for.

Today, many people make the mistake to blame what is going on in America on the American philosophy. I believe this is a double edge sword to the morals of us the Americans if we continue to practice this behavior. I am not saying this to tell you there is nothing wrong going on here. As a matter of fact, I believe something real horrible is wrong in our society. I feel, think and believe, and I should say I know there is something that is not right in our society. I know you have felt this also. And I know that you know the feeling which I am expressing. The feeling of being slaved and used. The feeling of having something stolen from us without having anybody to defend or represent us. The feeling that if you talk, you will become a target. The feeling of having the fear of being judged if you truly say what you believe. The feeling of having to hide your frustration with the government for the poor job they are doing. The feeling of having to be politically correct and staying apathetic to what is right but doing what is wrong. The feeling of losing our connection with all the other Americans, as we are isolated into our own cubicles. The feeling of having lost some of the most important values of being Americans. And all of that is because deep down inside, we know we have been hijacked, and we don't know what to do about it. We know the representatives we continuously have elected to be in the house have other interests rather than "our" best interest. They have, first and foremost, their own immediate selfish interest in mind, no matter who would be served and who would be hurt; and we don't say anything just because we don't like the alternative.

We are at a point where we have to wake up and make drastic changes to the way we live, the way we think, the way we make a living, the way we allow the government control us, the way we are fearful of the evil behind the politicians we have given power to, who surmount the white house, the congress, the house of Representatives, and the destructive financial institutes; all who have gained control over all of us. We need to wake up my friends, and the time for it is right now. Right now.

Although it was our naïve trust in the government that brought us to this point, we must not feel it is our own fault we have been taken as a hostage. Only if we become victims of this circumstance by doing nothing, then we have chosen to be victims of a Stockholm syndrome. That syndrome appears in the persons who have been kidnapped for a period of time by an abusive hijacker who brings them food everyday at the height of hunger. That sense of dependency causes a person who is taken to remain loyal to their hijacker. It keeps the taken stay "taken" even when the doors are open for them to free themselves. The blame does not remain with us for being taken a hostage, for being kidnapped. But if we know that there is a way out and we choose to stay "taken," then the blame remains with us. The door is right in front of us, and is still ajar.

We have a hope, and I am not talking about a false hope some charlatan politicians have promised us and then taken away from us. We all have seen the false hopes we have been given by so many smooth talking impostors calling themselves our representatives and leaders. No, no more of that. But a true hope. True hope is something we all have inside. It is not given to us by anyone, and so it cannot be taken away from us. I am talking about the light, the hope and the power that is within all of us who have come here from all over the world to call ourselves Americans. That is the hope.

For that reason, I have gathered the entire series of the weekly chronicles I wrote to my patients, concluding with a recent chapter to add to at the end, making this compilation as a book. I am writing you this book to just talk to you about some things I see that are going wrong in our land, this beautiful corner of the earth we call home. I am calling upon you to get up and clean house together. This message is to all of us who feel this land is our land; the beautiful land of America, the place once known as the vanguards of the revolutionary people, to put back our path onto the track of evolutionary progress.

AS THE PIRATES FOR DEMOCRACY QUIT

A few weeks back, I had a great conversation with one of our honorable patients, who is involved in protecting our society and assuring our safety from the recently discovered infection called "Global Terrorism." This conversation made me realize the need for all of us to talk with each other about the many issues that have revitalized and cultivated this monster we call terrorism. So, I want to share with you what I know and what I have observed as a doctor who would monitor and treat an infection when it spreads and damages its host. An infection would first target an organ, a region, and, if not treated as it populates in larger amounts, it would take control of the host's whole body, in our case of terrorism, the earth.

Before we get into what has happened in the past forty years in our world that has affected us today, especially in the Middle East, let's first recap and review the history of piracy, the most universally known commencement of terrorism in the world. That will help us understand how we got to the events of our daily lives today. At present, we humans are challenging each other with different ideologies and behaviors that have become the core of our belief systems. Those belief systems have brought comfort to the minds of the believers. However, such systems in return have separated societies in their justification of having a unique character and identity superior to others. Of course, the means to make one nation's identity strong and overbearing in relation to others is economic, namely money. And it is to obtain money that one group at a different level of life on earth always sees suppression of another group of people. This became the foundation and the beginning of a new world that was brought to life on the waters and gave rise to a new group of people called "pirates."

Pirates had long been traveling the waters of the Indian and Atlantic oceans. There were many French, Dutch, and English buccaneers' ships cruising the waters of the oceans carrying the flags of piracy.

Their income was obtained mainly from attacking and confiscating the valuables on the merchant ships of Spain, among others. Yet, it was only in about the seventeenth century that an organized society of pirates came to life. This coincided with the expansion of the Roman Catholic Church in Europe and the expansion of the Spanish fleet on waters exploiting Far East Asia and the western Americas' sources of commodities and goods.

Prior to the seventeenth century, Spain had become the great Catholic power of Europe, establishing itself as the leading colonial force in the Americas as well as the exploiters of Far East Asian resources. The remnants of such exploitation can be seen today in many Asian cultures, such as the Philippines. This colonial force of the Catholic Church had grown to such an extent that it attempted an invasion of the powerful nation of imperialist England in 1588, or the late sixteenth century. So England geared up.

England battled against the colonial power of Spain in the Indian and Atlantic oceans in the seventeenth century. The English government supported both privateering and piracy as means to combat and impair the Spanish fleet importing goods or deploying troops to various destinations. While piracy was considered terrorism and privateering was considered a respectable state policy, they both were given the needed support to combat the invasion of the Spanish Catholic Church by using brutal tactics. As a matter of fact, England's naval and merchant fleets concentrated their efforts on establishing and protecting English interests in Europe and India. Since Spain held almost all of the significant colonies in the West Indies and the South Pacific, the attacks of pirates and their journals of scientific information aided English interests.

England itself was suffering from rigid and hierarchical social structure. To many people, the way of life in piracy meant exploring life in freedom. This freedom took them away from the race, class, and gender segregation that were influencing their lives in England. And England itself was encouraging and supporting funds necessary to recruit less financially well-to-do citizens to join with pirates. Many pirates actually would gather enough wealth through their journeys to return to England and live among the higher-class population. Although pirates were known as brutal villains, many acted as ideal English citizens by publishing their discoveries in science and geography. Pirates provided nautical, geographical, ethnographic, and commercial data on the regions they had traveled to. Pirates were treated as honored citizens in return for the critical information they had brought to England to combat Spain. They also were credited with creating societies on board their ships that put in practice the democratic and classless ideals that were more accomplished than in the English colonies and England itself.

On the other hand, privateers who had official government commissions acted more ferociously in many ways than the pirates were believed to act. They greedily and selfishly traded slaves in cruel ways, exploited natural resources for a profit, and violently ignored and demolished the human rights of exploited indigenous people for profit. They did not act in the democratic ideology that pirates had created as fundamental rules for their societies on board the ships. Also, unlike the pirates, the seventeenth century privateers were authorized by the state of England and were obedient to its desires. Their "merchant vessels" were constructed much like warships, carrying cannons and trained crew to fight the Spanish war and merchant ships.

Many of the pirates returned to England to enjoy their newfound wealth through the development of plantations. However, upon their return, they found themselves back once again in the very familiar race, class, and gender suppressive society of England. The life of piracy they had lived had brought many of them the understanding of liberty, equality, and freedom of speech. Those were the fundamental rules onboard pirate ships, and such values were terribly missing in England. It was then that many decided to leave Europe behind to search of new territories where they could live freely. They moved to the New World.

Many people came to America in search of liberty, fairness, and equality. And they brought their money with them. Since many had had ties to England in their days of piracy, it seemed natural at first to accept the supervision of England over these new territories. After all, England had now defeated Spain and had posted a bounty against all remaining pirates. Since England now had become the superpower of the civilized world, it seemed to be most beneficial to remain allied with such a home base. However, England now was demanding high taxation on the hard work of the plantations of the new residents of America, the New World.

The rest, well, we know exactly what happened next. The colonies decided they wanted independence from the new power hungry superior imperialistic England. At this time, England had begun to expand its classist, racist, and gender segregationist thoughts back into the minds of the colonial population. The authorities of the English government would have the right to enter anyone's home at any time for inspection. The inspection was for money, arms, and goods that were not reported to English authorities. This inspection would take place at any time one might be suspected of losing loyalty or submission to the English authorities. Soon, a movement started to take shape among the colonists.

In the late 1700s, America had been home for some time to many philosophers, scientists, and politicians. Many of those educated people were nobles who had escaped the cruelty of the church and the suppression of European governments. They had brought their wealth to America and had developed plantations upon which the foundation of the economy of the New World was built. Many of those noble people had great ideas about how a democratic society should run. Such democratic societies had made a nation previously on the waters of the oceans. One of those noble people who changed the lives of humanity forever was Thomas Jefferson, the founding father who brought to life the Declaration of Independence that later became the foundation for the Constitution of the United States of America. Today, a spreading danger infesting our own government has put the existence of the spirit of Declaration of Independence into jeopardy.

Perhaps the thought of this spreading danger might sound a bit far-fetched to you. After all, many of us surprisingly behave as if the world still is flat! We have traditionally thought, if we walk long enough, we can always walk away from our problems. Or, at least, that is how our so-called social and spiritual leaders tend to behave in response to the very problem we have encountered for hundreds of years. But, before I get ahead of myself, I have to tell you that this will be a very long conversation, and I promise to deliver my message to you in the upcoming weekly issues if you can be patient.

I will review the history of humankind with you to clarify the connections George W. Bush has had with true terrorism, and how such connections are detrimental to our ideology and the evolution of the Declaration of Independence. I would also like to reveal how the politicians coming into power after Bush are going to continue this path of decay of the Constitution. What I ask right now is for you to be patient, open-minded and focused on what we all want from the life we are living as Americans: Liberty and Justice for All.

REVOLUTION CONTINUES

It was a quiet and rather warm afternoon sailing on the Mediterranean Sea in the early spring of 1801. The sea was calm. There didn't seem to be any reason why a well-trained crew on a well-made ship should not enjoy such a warm sunny afternoon drinking wine and getting tan. But the men on the ship were restless, worried, and anxious. The wind against the flapping flag was the only sound you could hear, which did not take the focus away from the quiet sail on the water. As one looked closely at the crew, one could see they all were looking at the same point a distance ahead. There was a ship ahead posting no flag other than one raised later on—it was the flag known among the pirates. This was a Muslim pirate ship they were quietly chasing.

This naval ship was one of the first American vessels to enter the Mediterranean Sea to hunt and combat Muslim pirate ships. Muslim piracy was a cause of terror for merchants, businessmen and women from Europe and America traveling on the seas. This infection on the seas was the result of the corruption the Muslim pirates had brought to the Mediterranean south of Europe, as well as partial or non-Muslim pirates to the Caribbean by the lands of the Americas. Piracy had remained a source of income for Muslim countries such as the Ottoman Empire, Tunis, Tripoli, Algiers, and parts of Morocco. And prior to March of 1801 and before the American navy, there was no organized navy to combat pirates. The mission of this American vessel, USS Enterprise and her crew was to combat the infection that was expanding forward and now nearing America. And the fighting ships USS Constitution, Constellation, Philadelphia, Chesapeake, Argus, Syren, and Intrepid had gone into war on waters and ashore on the home lands of the pirates. They had reached the edges of the Middle East and North Africa, where Westerners were kept as hostages and slaves. This became the first battle in which the U.S. flag was carried and planted overseas.

The war soon started as the American navy vessel reached a firing distance behind the pirates' ship. This war continued for months and years to come on the shores of Tripoli and the Ottoman Empire and other Muslim countries, until they surrendered to the American marines who landed and conquered and brought the Muslims into signing a treaty with the U.S. This was not an easy treaty to reach. England was offering the Turkish pirates much support and encouragement to fight America, England's new enemy. Despite the treaty, the war of the Muslims against America soon was declared to be the jihad that Mohammad, the creator of Islam, told his people to prepare for more than one millennium ago. It was the beginning of a war that would last centuries. The time had now arrived for Muslims to acknowledge and prepare to confront the "infidel," the enemy they had been warned to be wary of by their leader, the Prophet Mohammad. The chess game started with Muslims and anti-American ideology on one side and American ideology on the other. This was the cause all Muslims needed to find a focus for their union, to rise against what they saw as the enemy of Islam, America. Although this game gained complexity on both sides at this time as it went forward, the hostility of the Muslim world towards America had started just after America's separation from England took place. And the goal of the game for the Muslim side under the guidance of England ever since has been to destroy America by all means. Of course, England would reach its goal of winning back a lost battle with America if Muslims would bring the new young strong country down to her knees.

The guidance of Muslims in war against America by England became clear to America when in 1786, Jefferson, then the American ambassador to France, and Adams, then the American ambassador to Britain met in London with Sidi Haji Abdul Rahman Adja, the ambassador of Tripoli/Algiers. They asked him simply why the Muslim nations were holding such hostility against a new nation with which they had no previous contacts.

The ambassador replied, "Islam was founded on the laws of their prophet, and that it was written in their Quran, that all the nations which had not acknowledged the authority of the prophet were sinners, whom it was the right and duty of the faithful to plunder and enslave wherever they could be found." However, Muslims did not recognize England as such enemy.

For about 200 years, the problem seemed to have gone dormant in the Middle East. The pirates had lost their ships and power of maneuverability on the seas. The world had gone through two devastating global wars among many local ones. America had helped free Europe and England from subjugation under a bloody dictator. America helped England and France to back the major targeted victims of World War II to situate and form a country called Israel. The union of the Muslim nations was disturbed by the connections and the influence America had achieved through the strong U.S.-backed army of the Pahlavi dynasty in Iran and the government of Israel. Iran became the main ally, a fuel provider and a base for American presence in the center of the Middle East. The Middle East appeared to be under control and in favor of America. If only that control would remain intact for another twenty years…but England was not happy.

In essence, England had picked up the strategy that once before appeared so successful in defeating enemies. Soon after the loss of its American colonies, England supported a new line of pirates. These

new pirates were the very Turkish Muslim pirates of the Mediterranean Sea, and the target was American merchant ships and any other merchant ships that would trade with the American economy. You might wonder why and when America became the Great Satan in the eyes of Middle Eastern cultures. The answer has been right in front of us all along, but we have not paid enough attention. England has sided with Middle Eastern cultures for more than two centuries, warning them about the evil that will come from America, the Great Satan. We are now fighting a war in the Middle East blindfolded in this year of 2006. And we do not comprehend that the hand that is holding the blindfold on our eyes is that of the ally who is pushing and encouraging us to enter into this battle. But why is England conducting such a calculated plan and holding such grudge over the losing battles against America?

War did not appear to be a winning key to England whenever the direct opponent has been America. The war wasn't a good idea when the colonies revolted in the late 1700s. It wasn't a good idea in the War of 1812. And most certainly it wasn't a good idea for England when competing internationally with the new American culture, industry, and wealth. So, a new war had to be designed, a war that would disable the economy and the spirit of the America. But what could be the winning strategy that not only would weaken the unruly child that England once resented having lost, but also would remove the one flaw in the England's plans of victory over the world. You see, such plans were placed into action many centuries ago. And the plans were going to proceed just fine if it wasn't for America.

MOMENTUM OF THE PRESENCE

Well, let us first talk about Britain and who Britons are. About 3,000 years ago, a highly civilized group of people from the Phoenician region started navigating the waters of the Mediterranean Sea and out into the Atlantic along the cost of Western Europe and into the island of Briton. The Phoenicians invaded the island of Briton in 1103 BC. The Phoenician pioneers were not Semites but appeared to be most likely Aryan and Celtic in origin. Soon, they settled on the island in search of tin mines; they found the island to be inhabited by Picts. Picts were considered to be aborigines, a primitive people from eastern Asia Minor and Mesopotamia in the Stone Age. As time went on, the two groups intermarried and the population of Britons grew.

There is, however, a difference between the origin of British and English people. The English people are Anglo-Saxons from Germany who came to the British Isles in the fifth century. Here is what happened that brought the Anglo-Saxons. By 400 AD, despite much resistance among the population, Britons had become a part of the Roman Empire. In return, the Roman Empire promised the Britons what they had sought for many years—protection from the terrorist groups belonging to the neighboring Germanic territories. However, by 406 AD, due to the costly local wars, the Roman legions that were the protectors of the island against the Germanic pirates and raiders from the north and Wales left the islands. Britons had no choice but to look for alternative options for protection.

Since Britons needed a more warlike people, they invited the Saxons, a Germanic people, including the Germanic pirates. They also invited Angles, another Germanic people, from north of Saxon's original home. Angles and Saxons soon dominated the local Roman population, so Britons later took an Anglo-Saxon identity. As this transformation took place, the island eventually was called "Anglia." Then it became "Angle land," which turned into "Angland," and eventually pronounced "England." Subjugation of Britons also initi-ated a resistance among a population that moved north into the island. That is when England put into effect a series of policies to fight the resistance. England also devised tactics to be practiced for many gen-erations to come, to rule the world as they have known it. England has long been familiar with utilizing clandestine relations with regional pirates for the purposes of protection against and domination of resis-tance forces.

The American Revolution actually was a revolutionary war of Brit-ish colonial citizens who migrated from their island into the New World and then rebelled against their government, wanting indepen-dence from an English society filled with rules of racial and class seg-regation. That is one of the major differences between British and English people. This is how the English government lost America, the largest investment ever in its history, to the British colonists who later became Americans. England not only wants but also needs to recover this loss.

In spite of everything, the seasoned England banks on a major phil-osophical difference that separated it from the young and inexperi-enced America. Today, England is acting upon this major difference. You are asking what that difference may be. We all know this very fundamental difference between the two, but I believe we all take it very lightly to a point where we do not acknowledge its existence and importance. Here is what that difference is: You see, as much as we Americans believe in uniting people under one system of justice to reach the stars above, England believes in dividing people of the world and conquering them down here on earth. The separation of philosophies is the very important fundamental difference between our two societies.

This difference is the foundation of an old vision that has separated the humans who have a vision of seeking the truth from humans who suppress and hide the truth. That is to say, the American vision and spirit is one that seeks the truth regardless of the power of the author-ities, while the English vision is to deceive and trick, to remain as the authority that one day will have to guide, protect, and rule the world under its exploitation and heavy taxation. Let me explain the other side of the coin that separates us from England.

The liberty-seeking people throughout ages have learned the value and necessity of financial independence to support their freedom. One of the most successful revolutions in the history of liberty-seeking humans has been the American Revolution against the English. The most important factor for such success was the American belief in the "momentum of the presence." Let me make it clearer. The momentum of our presence is the reason, the drive, and the belief that we all live for, work for, and fight for.

Although such beliefs, reason, and drive could seem to have dissimilarities in different cultures, they are fundamentally the same among all freedom-seeking humanity. That momentum of the presence is not having a luxury car or buying a big house. It is not the number of playthings we can accumulate around us in the shortest amount of time. It is not how nice our clothes are and how young and beautiful we can keep ourselves for years to come. And, most certainly, it is not how many advanced electronic devices we can afford to get our children. Those are all the things we'd like to have. The momentum of our presence is something that is far beyond all the things we'd like to have. And all that we'd like to have is the gifts—a result of the very foundation we live for. Our momentum of the presence, what we Americans fight and live for, is the Constitution that has been born from the evolutionary experiment of humanity, the noble Declaration of Independence of the United States of America.

THE INTENT AND THE FOCUS

In this issue, I will share with you a few paragraphs from my book, *Pi, a Pathway to Life*. I wrote the following paragraphs at the turn of the century as we approached and entered the year 2000. I want you to take a few moments, take a breather, and then go back in time. Not too far back; only a few years back. To be exact, I want you to remember what you were doing in 2000, where you traveled to, what movies you saw in the theater, what you did that made that time special. I need you to reach that nostalgic moment before continuing. If you are not ready to do this yet, then please wait until you can. If you are prepared and have the opportunity, then stop reading and go and reach the nostalgia first. And please, no cheating!

So, if you are ready, here we go...

The year is 2000. This year, I traveled to many places to see what was going on around the world, and this year I went back to Iran after such a long time. It was interesting what I saw with my own eyes. Throughout my traveling, I continuously remembered what one of the greatest philosophers of the past hundred years predicted about the last twenty years of the twentieth century. This noble philosopher predicted that in that period of time closer to the year 2000, humanity would experience a new level of philosophical revolution, a revolution through which the planet comes into contact with many progressive jumps in spirituality that surpass the areas of economical, political, scientific, and industrial revolutions of the past centuries. The scientific and industrial revolutions of the eighteenth, nineteenth, and twentieth centuries become the supporting grounds for the great jump in the evolution of mental and philosophical levels of humanity—levels unprecedented in the history of humanity.

It is fascinating to see how this prediction has come true in many parts of the world. As one travels throughout the world, one can see the progression of the evolution of humanity taking different levels of alacrity in accordance with the scientific and industrial supporting bases they have provided for their societies. Those societies that have concentrated on such progressive philosophy have indeed taken great steps in that direction toward such destinations. The year 2000 has become the summit of the progression in the revolution of the mental and spiritual activities of humanity in many parts of the world. And this is when I visited Iran. As I said before, what I found in Iran was an eye-opening experience that had an immense effect on my understanding of what is taking place in that part of the world.

I have always believed in the value of the notion: "Whatever we focus on with our intentions is what we receive from the universe." The dark age of the year 2000 definitely was present in Iran. This was a future that was predicted, expected, and practiced by the people in Iran since many years ago. The heartfelt emotions through popular songs that were reaching the lives of many in Iran had brought them to the exact destination. A fear and panic that conducted the people to making hasty decisions led them in a direction of life that was exactly what frightened them. And such terror now exists in every corner of life in Iran.

This fear, however, seems to be a global fright that we humans have dealt with for the past 2,000 years. We can see that, as humans, we have prepared ourselves for so long for a point in the future to fight against an invading force that can threaten our purpose in life, our existence, and our evolution in the direction we have chosen. In many religions, they talk about doomsday, or Armageddon. In many predictions, visionaries have expressed the time when the world faces a great battle—a battle that leaves very few survivors—a "day of judgment" when we would distinguish between the believers and the nonbelievers. And this judgment day appears to be around 2000 or the twenty-first century in the scripts of many.

Why do most prophecies predict such common doomsdays so uniformly? It seems there is no real scientific reason why this time in human history should be so crucial and important to why such a great battle must take place. There is no real consequence that brought the need for this encounter, except that, perhaps, like any other project to be completed, humans need a deadline for themselves to reach a specific level of evolution. It could be that this is a motivational tool to push everyone to reach the height of their understanding and power in

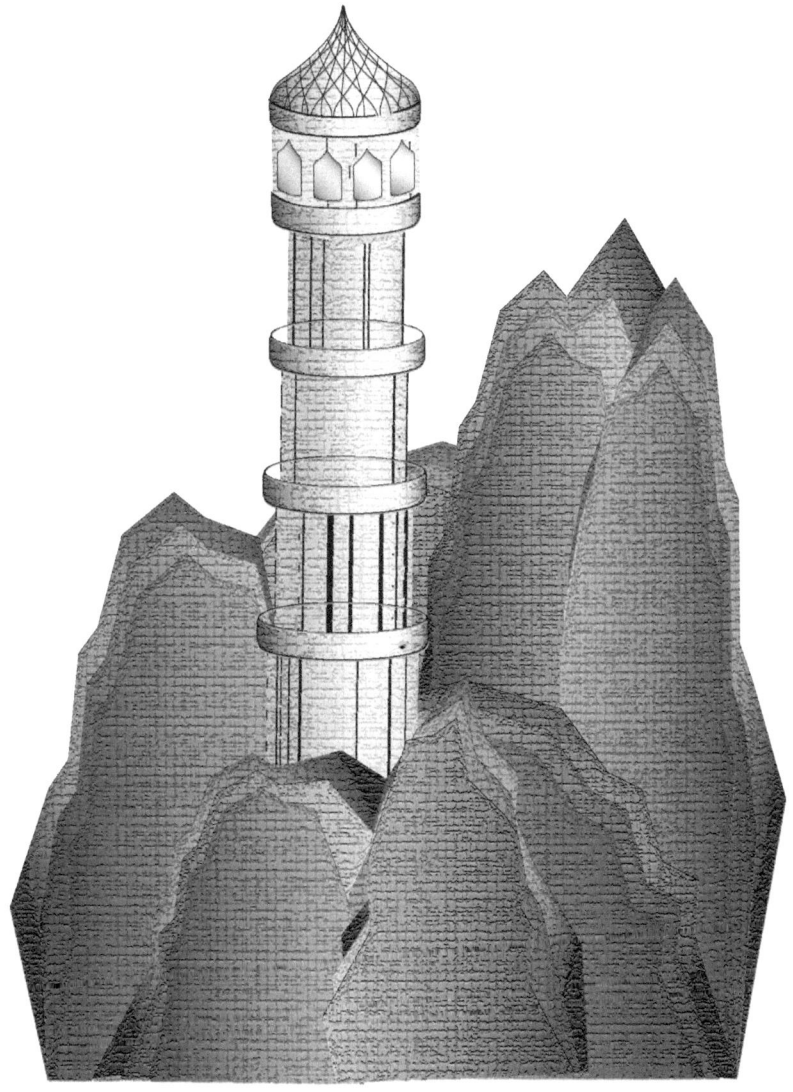

the path in life they have chosen to grow within. Perhaps we were given a deadline to have a focus.

Think of a high school with many students attending. They are all sitting in the class trying to be as proper as teenagers can be sitting on a hard seat for an hour or so. They are all waiting for the recess bell to ring. And, as soon as the bell rings, everyone is rushing out of the class, destroying all the order that was in place in the classroom. There seems to be nothing different about the school or the students who are attending the schools between the times they are in the class or when they are on the schoolyard or the cafeteria, except for the attitude of the students. It isn't because something is happening in the yard. It is rather because of what the students want to happen when they are out of the classroom. It is the same for us humans with the year 2000. The time of the millennium is important, not because something is going to happen, rather because we as humans want something to happen.

Religious leaders talk about "Judgment Day" when a prophet or a descendant returns to take the believers back to heaven. And the nonbelievers would go to the land of the oblivious. Visionary storytellers have predicted the time when a nation is going to start a war in the Middle East and when another nation is going to take over the world afterward. And scientific sources have talked about the problems we will face by the development of the computers as we have.

Perhaps all of that could take place in one form or another, not because we are distant to receive this future, but because we are focusing on such a chain of events that we eventually will reach that destination in our future history. I call it a "history" because we have made plans in the past for that future to happen ahead of us. That makes the events ahead of us behave as something that already has been lived in the past. Soon we will see the computers taking control over our lives. The nations in the Middle East start thinking it is now their time to rebel and to gain power by unifying. For some of the leaders in this area, they start feeling they are the promised messiah, the messenger from God to save people and the world. Such leaders soon will be defined between the believers and the nonbelievers. Such leaders soon will try to distinguish between the ones who are with them and the ones who are against them.

It all can happen, not because it has to happen, but because we have planned for it to happen. Perhaps we need this chain of events to happen because we have reached a point where we do not have enough reason to put up with each other's differences. Perhaps it is time to break away from our supporting grounds and make an attempt to reach higher levels of existence and thinking, where religions and superstitions do not rule our minds and lives. Perhaps we have prepared ourselves for the day when we need to make a choice to either continue our path of evolution and jump to a higher level or kill each other to the point of extinction because of our own man-made rules and superstitions, religions, and traditions that would prevent us from growing—the same rules and religions that we created once before to protect us from outside danger. The only matter that could stop us from making a terrible choice that would result in such destiny would be a greater danger that would threaten the survival of all humanity at once.

The truth is that the year 2000 was the dawn of the higher thoughts in matters spiritual and philosophical, social, political, economical, scientific, and industrial all around the world. As we approached the turn of the century, an assumption brought about a fear around the world that the global changes had taken place too quickly. The changes were believed to be so radical that the world could not bear them once the turn of the century would arrive. That year came by and left us before we even had a chance to focus on it for long. Perhaps you might remember how some people were so concerned about the turn of the century that they changed their whole lives around to be prepared for the malfunction of the whole world as we knew it. And what they got at the end was the unpleasant sensation of loss as a result of the unfavorable changes they made in their own lives. Those people have been at work on their destructive path ever since.

Although this year became the symbol of constructive changes for the majority of the world, it became the dark ages the Iranian people had expected. And who made such dark ages for them, or for anybody else? No one but themselves and by the help of the influence of popular Iranian pop singers such as Darioush and other songwriters and poets and writers like him. Such ill-minded artists became very popular in the mid-1970s. These artists were the ones who directed a generation, a society, and a future of the world into a destructive and self-sabotaging path by their wrongful utilization of the power of art and its influences in people's lives. The infection was a point of morose and sullen focus that turned the new generation of Iranians against the Western world. A series of so-called artworks infected the minds of the young and growing generations of Iranians grew to distrust and resent the Western influences and changes that were replacing the old and unwell ways of traditional Iranian thinking. The work of such so-called artists was nothing but a cry for help and regret in the world of sorrow and loss they shared with others. The effects of their work could be compared to the effects of some artists like Kurt Cobain of Nirvana who brought the unwell grunge movement into our American society in the 1990s.

Nevertheless, and no matter what happened before us, we are here at this time of history facing the global problems we have tried to ignore for so long—the problems we stayed away from but kept in proximity to gain profit from. We remained as beneficiary bystanders of such battles, and now we have been pulled in and have become involved. We have become a part of the problem by becoming involved in the war that is going on in the global battle. The decisions we make on this battlefield will influence the future of the next generations. We need to recognize what we have become involved in and what part we are holding in this massive chaos.

Now is the time we need to acknowledge the power and responsibility that have been invested in us by making decisive steps into a future where we want to provide for the destiny of humanity. It is the present time when we need to reevaluate the direction of the influence of the songwriters and the influences of the artists of our societies on us on an individual basis. We need to reconsider the authorities we choose to direct us into the future. We need to remember the voices of the founding fathers when they chanted for separation of church and state. We need to become aware individually of the effects of such influences on our lives. I do not mean that we should limit the self-expression of ourselves and the society by the rulings of an authority. Rather, what I mean is that each of us individually has to make a decision and acknowledge how the way we occupy our time can influence our future. We need to make this decision actively for ourselves. If we become passive to the judgment of the ruling parties of any society, then we have condemned ourselves to follow the same path of destiny many other broken-down societies have gone through.

INDEED THEY STARTED ON THE WRONG FOOT

Do you want to know why we cannot understand the world of the Middle East? Or why the Arabic world cannot understand us? Do you want to know the fundamental difference that has separated us from each other that has made us incapable of understanding each other's worlds? And do you want to know when we separated as humans to grow so far apart in our ways of living this life on earth? It is much simpler than we have thought and tried to explain. And I will share with you a simple reason that cannot be understood by the very Arabic-oriented ways of thinking. But first, let me tell you a short story.

A few months ago, I was in a crowd of Arabic-oriented people, mostly Iranians. Now, I have to share with you that Iranians do not like to be called Arabs. And they try to separate themselves from Arabs based on the historical events that took place 4,000 years ago in the land of Parthian, what we now call Iran. After our discussion in this paper, perhaps it will become clearer why Iranians are a part of the Arabic society of the Middle East, and how we need to deal with them accordingly.

Back to our story: I was hopelessly trying to make a point to this crowd of mostly Iranians that as long as they do what they have been doing the same way for thousands of years, they will receive nothing but what they have received for all this time. And what is it that they have received throughout history? A series of misfortunes, painful results, and a miserable social life that is based on scarcity. Well, needless to say, they all were offended. "How dare you say that life in Iran is miserable?" My answer to them was a question: If life in Iran is not miserable, then what are you doing living in this part of the world. Their response as always was that Iran is not a friendly place to them right now because of the mullahs who are running the country. They also responded that most or nearly all Iranians in or out of Iran are subjugated by those mullahs. My question again: If you love

Iran so much, why are you not there changing what you do not like? Their response was that they could not change the situations in Iran because the force of the mullahs is too great for all Iranians to confront and change. My next question: Where did such power come from? The response is what we always hear from Iranians: "It is the West that is supporting and providing power to the mullahs!"

What was not clear to me, and perhaps is a question in your mind also, is how a whole country could be subjugated by a conspiracy of the Western world when they all know about such conspiracy? Perhaps the logic I was using was not sufficient for the sake of argument. I tried to dig into the logic to understand the connection that was missing or a barrier that was separating us.

Now, what causes such separation is what needs to be changed if we want to have any future in the world as one living, breathing planet. So I looked and searched for the possible reasons why we have developed so differently in such a small world. I found something that grabbed my attention, so I followed the lead, and that took me to a light that shined upon my path of searching for the truth. I will share with you what I have found to be such an important factor; let me tell you a bit about the alphabet I am using in this paper that facilitates our communication on a visual level. It is called an essay consisting of words—words based on alphabets.

And because the quality of the life we are living is based only on the words we are using in relation to each other, it is important to know where those words have come from—the words are compilations of different alphabets. Let's see where today's alphabet came from. The Latin alphabet that we are using to write and read this paper comes from the Greek alphabet that is based on the Phoenician alphabet. The letters in the Latin (or Roman) alphabet have their origins in pictogram. "What the heck is a pictogram?" you might ask. A pictogram is "a symbol representing a concept, object, activity, or a place or event by illustration. Pictography is a form of writing whereby ideas are transmitted through drawing. It is the basis of hieroglyphs and cuneiform." (Hieroglyphs are the parent to Egyptian writings and cuneiform is the Sumerian alphabet parent to the old Persian writing alphabet that no longer exists.)

Let me explain how a pictogram works. When you are running down the hallway looking for a sign that shows you where the restroom is, you are looking at a pictogram. Or when you are in a city trying to catch a flight and you look for the sign that guides you to the

Proto-Canaanite	Phoenician	Value and name	Descendants
𓃾	𐤀	ʾ ʾalp "ox"	א A A
⊓	𐤁	b bet "house"	ב B B ب
⌐	𐤂	g gaml "throwstick"	ﭖ Γ C-G ج
𓆛 ⊓	𐤃	d digg "fish"	ﻰ Δ D ذ-د
𓀠	𐤄	h haw / hll "hurrah"	ה E E є Є
♀	Y	w waw "hook"	ו F-Y F-U-V-W-Y و
=	I	z zen / ziqq "handcuff"	ﺮ Z Z ز 3
Ⅲ	日	ḥ ḥet "courtyard"	ﺢ H H خ-ح
⊕	⊗	ṭ ṭēt "wheel"	ﻭ Θ ظ-ط ﻮ
↳	⅄	y yad "arm"	ﻱ I I-J ي
Ш	𐤊	k kap "hand"	כ K K ك
ℂ	︿	l lamd "goad"	ל Λ L ﻝ
∼∼∼	⅏	m mem "water"	מ M M م
ﮯ	𐤍	n naḥš "snake"	Nun N N ن
≢ ‡	‡	s samek "fish"	ס Ξ X 𝄵
⊙	O	ʿ ʿen "eye"	ﻉ O O ع-ﻍ
ﺝ	⍵	p piʾt "bend"	פ Π P ف ﻑ
‖ ﬨ	ﬧ	ṣ ṣad "plant"	ﺺ м ﺺ-ﺽ Ц
8	φ	q qup "monkey"	ק Q Q ﻕ ϛ
𝕬	𐤓	r raʾs "head"	ﺮ P R ر
⍵	W	š/ś šimš "sun, the Uraeus"	ﺵ Σ S ش-س Ш
+	+	t taw "signature"	ﬨ T T ت-ث

airport, you are after the pictogram for traveling on a plane. Those are pictures that resemble what they signify: a place, an action, or a need. Simple pictograms started to become a system of communication about 11,000 years ago among farmers. As urban revolution[1] took place about 8,000 years ago, the system of pictograms became more complex and descriptive. At this point, the pictographic system became the logographic writing system.

So the alphabets represent a meaning or an entity on their own. For instance, in the parent writing system of the Phoenician alphabet, letter "A" represents an ox, "B" is the representative for house, "C" is for throw stick, "D" is for fish, and so on. This system is the parent to many other alphabets in different languages. The Phoenician alphabet gave rise to the Greek, Latin, Hebrew, Farsi, and Arabic alphabets. At this point of the urban revolution, the Phoenician alphabet was missing a crucial part, which was corrected by the Greeks. The missing substance in the Phoenician alphabet was that vowels were not symbolized within the alphabets as letters. Greeks added symbols for such vowels, which jump-started the evolution of Western civilization. The Farsi and Arabic alphabets did not correct the situation in the same matter and relied only on placing accents above or below a letter to give it a sense of vowel. In other words, in Arabic writing, there are no letters for the sounds of "e" as in fest or "a" as in fast. You would only know if the word in a sentence is a fest or fast in context of the other words in the sentence. And if you ask how they would know the word is—for sake of argument—fest or fast, they would look at you with ridicule and respond, "How could you not know?"

Yes, they might have a point there, that, when you are talking about a clear matter or situation, of course you would know if the word is fest as compared to fast. But what about situations where you are invited to a fest and on the invitation all they write is F S T, and you think they are asking you to fast. Is this important? You bet it is. I want to offer an example and I hope you will stick with me as I try to describe it by drawing on a piece of paper. So, please grab a piece of paper and draw a symbol for the words RUN, ALERT, BURNING, JUNGLE, AHEAD. You can draw whatever symbol you want for

---

[1] Urban revolution took place when the farmers gathered to create cities with laws and governing systems. Poetry, philosophy, and gathering of information are the characteristics of this new era. Please refer to my book, *Pi, a Pathway to Life* for further explanation.

them. The symbols are not important. What we are going to do with them is important.

Now, imagine there is a word for the pictogram of such event, and put it into a writing pictographic system that would read "RABJA." So, as soon as you would see the symbol RABJA, you would know what is going on and what to do. You basically know there is a vast fire ahead that probably has blocked the road you are on, and you need to find a new road to run away from the fire ahead. Now, I want you to take away the entire vowel in this pictogram, as it appears to be unnecessary in the Farsi and Arabic alphabets. What you end up with is the pictogram "RBJ," which tells you to run from the burning jungle with no other clarifying information. Worse yet, one might want to add his or her own vowels such as "U" for unprepared and "O" for on the side and you get the pictogram symbol RUBJO. In this case, because of the lack of vowels, one might mistakenly run straight forward with no other precautions to respond to the unclear RBJ sign. Chances are that since you do not know you have to be alert about what is ahead, you will end up running directly into the fire! What makes a difference is the clarity that remains in or is taken away from a description.

This implementation of clarity made a great difference between young societies that initiated their communication from the same parenting alphabetic system. One made the system more complete, resulting in facilitation of the evolution of the social philosophy and logic; the others ran around in chaos trying to survive the disasters that were put in their way by outside forces. One became the vanguard to logical thinking; the other became the victim of unruliness and frustration. One became the scientific effort to reach space; the other just prays to the imaginary forces in space.

The Arabic nation is where communication is done by the same chaotic system of alphabets. Such societies lack logic and sophistication from the evolution of their cultures. They have continued to exist merely as great survivors that have learned to live within a chaos only by changing direction when they get to the obstruction that confronts them, with no sense of direction or improvement. This is their way of existence, and the current population is the offspring of all who, throughout generations, could run, at best, violently with no respect or understanding of the Greek method of ideology and philosophy. What happened that brought the Arabic societies to such condemnation is the limitation they created for themselves when describing their situation and their environment to each other and other societies.

The reason is the historical factor that they either would not communicate new situations and findings via descriptive pictograms or, when they did face the fact, that they might misunderstand each other. How could one have a truly logical conversation with people who have evolved to be illogical?

All we know is that we need to change this or else we will all be troubled by the frantic, aimless, terrified runners who are willing to knock down everything in front of them without understanding the necessity to find solutions to the problems around to make our small planet a place to live for all of us. In their illogical brains, they even justify that, if they cannot put out the fire, at least they can wrap a bomb around themselves to go to heaven when they blow up everyone else for whom they blame the fire.

THE CARROT

Today let's talk about the most booming business of our era and our time, the first decade of twenty-first century—real estate. I cannot call it an industry, because it actually is not a wheel that will move us forward in the long run. This line of business needs nothing but greed for one to be a part of it. Everyone is going nuts over it. The Realtors are doing very well with such a bubble inflating our economy. The construction companies are not making enough buildings and not building fast enough. One could not go wrong quitting a job to get a license to a sell real estate. I mean, a 3 percent commission on a $500,000 house is $15,000. A person needs to sell only five houses a year to live a comfortable life—a life much more comfortable than a person like me who works real hard every day to serve society. So, guess what is more appealing?

This movement of easy money throughout society is an alarming fad that is only going to hurt us in the long run. Everyone is eager to see the price of housing go up like a rocket, because everyone thinks they are going to make money. As a matter of fact, it does look very convincing, and I guess you have to be a fool not to be a part of it, huh? After all, which fool would turn his or her back on such easy income? If you don't do it, there are so many others who will take advantage of this opportunity and leave you behind in your own world of ethics and morals, right?

Well, there is another side to it. As we leave our posts in society, our economy relies on the over inflation of real estate. It is easy to overinflate housing prices because we are growing exponentially in population, and everyone needs a house. So, we have made it very easy for everyone to get a loan. No matter how much a person makes, no matter if people can truly afford a house or not, some company will approve a loan based on inaccurate information and documents. And everyone loves it, because the loan officers advertise and give

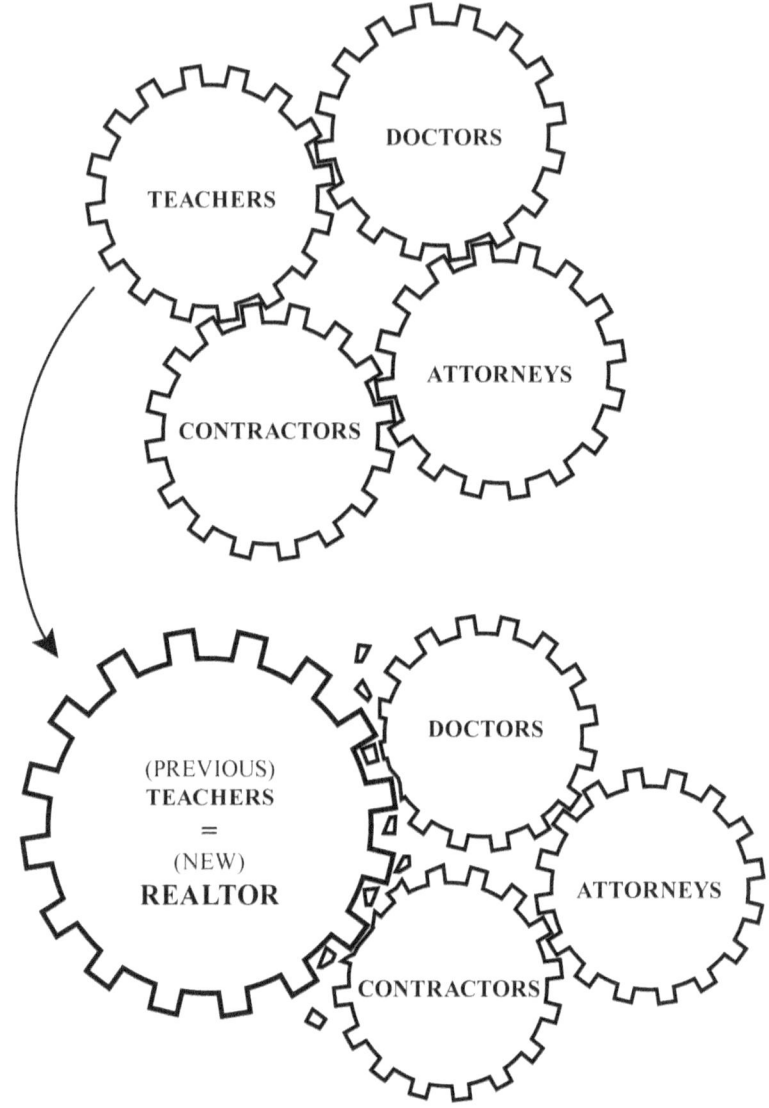

hope to the lenders that the price of housing will rise again, and everyone can refinance again and again and again. Well, when is it all going to hit the wall, the bottom, and the fan?

This easy money train will create a society full of people who become more and more lazy, and more and more addicted to such easy money and the toys that come along as the reward for such subordination. It is a voluntary slavery that is invading our society. And we are all falling for it. Guess what? Everyone wants to be Donald

Trump. And the price for it, yes, is right. "Just give up your skills, your job, and your position in the society, get your Realtor's license and we will make it easy for you. That is all it takes. You will make money, will be comfortable, will have the car you want with all the gas you wish to burn; go ahead and buy a couple of the properties for yourself, refinance a couple of times, and make a little bit more money on that, and live happily ever after. Don't worry; you do not need to know where the money comes from. Just enjoy it, at least for now."

Yes, we don't have to worry about it now. As a matter of fact, we are told to just go with the flow. We will worry about the consequences later. Well, let me tell you, my friends, this is a very dangerous behavior to practice. What we will get at the end is a society broken into shambles as a result of the dislocation of its key members lost in the cyberspace and real estate chaos. And this is how it is going to happen.

Real estate is the backing of our economy. If we intend to overinflate the very supporting ground that is holding our economy on the top levels globally, soon we will raise the price of the housing beyond our own affordability. Ground is only supporting so long as it remains beneath us; otherwise, it will become a burial site. Think about that for a few minutes. Once the supporting ground has risen to any extent, all other components of the society that revolve around and above this holding ground must remain on top of it in order to survive.

The price of food will go up. The price of gas will go up. The price of metal will go up. If the automobile industry is planning to survive in the long run, it will have to raise prices or go to the bare minimum. The price of our speeding and parking tickets will go up. The number of the inmates in the prisons will exceed the capacity. And the price of water will be higher than oil. Energy costs will rise and, as a result, electricity will be very expensive to maintain. Our economy will try to stay above this for the next few years, until the exhausted system collapses under its own weight. And that is when help is going to arrive. But beware of those who are on the side of help. Because, if you look very carefully, underneath it all, you will see the redcoats once again.

England will come to help. England will be the rescuer, the hero that is going to bail out our imploded banking system. And you and I probably are not going to do anything about it. We will just sit back and watch as the rug is pulled out right from beneath us. Why?

Because we are so busy standing in line for the new electronic toys that are going to be released we want to be the first to have one. Because they tell us if you have one, then you are the coolest, and all others are losers. Our own White House cabinet is the mob taking our livelihoods away from us. They feed us the lines and we take them. In the process, we are so busy with this race for the new toys that we fail to see they are taking our house away from us—our house, our United States of America, our Constitution, our Declaration of Independence, our revolution, and freedom.

WHAT IS GOOD FOR ME HAS TO BE GOOD FOR ALL OF US

After writing and distributing last week's article, my staff advised me that perhaps I should tone down the articulation of my thoughts. After all, my staff reminded me that a lot of people are supporters of the Bush cabinet and would be offended by my comments. Also, many people who are involved with the real estate overload do not see it the way I do, and, perhaps, I would lose credibility with them.

My friends let me tell you something: I hope I am wrong. I hope time will prove me wrong. I hope we are not sold out to the rest of the world that is not happy with our freedom, although I believe there will be a time when we will have to stand our grounds against the rest of the world. I hope we do not have to compromise our values and our independence in the future when we encounter the trillions of dollars owed to the very institutions we have fought against for so long. But if we find ourselves at that point, wouldn't it be a shame if I had known something and I didn't tell you?

I'll take the risk that you won't like what I am saying. I also hope that if I do say it now, we can make some changes and avoid that downfall altogether. Let me remind you, we are at war—a very costly war that will drag us down with its hunger for money. So far, we have spent many billions of dollars in this war, and we are not clear where the money is going. But I believe we are not going to do anything about this missing money until it passes a trillion dollars of spending no one can account for. That is the time our banks are going to collapse, our industries are going to be sold out to foreign investors, our real estate economy is going to burst, and our freedom is going to be compromised.

It is so interesting to see how most people delude themselves into believing they have no part in the problems that occur in their lives. Most people blame others or the world around them for what is wrong in their lives. Most people do not realize that if something is wrong in their lives or in their society, that itself is a reflection of their actions and behavior. Some people do not even see the need to change anything in their lives. And some others are aware of the mistakes they make but are adamant about accepting their mistakes as such. I have just one request: free yourself. Open up your heart to whom you really are. Open up your heart to your desires. And open up your heart to your soul. Open your mind's eye.

We have to be aware of the focus in our lives. We have to acknowledge why we do what we are doing in our daily lives. We need to know if it is only a force of norm and habit that is making us get up in the morning, dress, and go to work, or if there is some other force beyond daily existence. Why are we doctors, attorneys, teachers, drivers, waiters, chefs, engineers, pilots, cabinet secretaries or the president? What is it that connects us all to work toward a goal that appears to be common? And what is the drive in us that is the source of our actions?

Is it that we have a purpose, a direction in life that is making every breath we take a miracle of the universe? There seems to be a drive that affects every organism that exists in the universe.

It is having that purpose in life that gives every breath we take a meaning. It is that purpose that can give us the energy to look for the right ways to do things—the right ways that can bring us the prosperity we all long for deep inside, the prosperity that is sought via so many different avenues. Some seek it in money. Some try to catch it with alcohol or drugs. Some just like toys to occupy them and do anything to get the new "things" as soon as they are out in the market. Some think they can reach a source of connection by having many sexual partners. Some turn their credulous minds to accepting a dogma and following blindly. Although all could be a vehicle to higher levels at times, they often are mistaken for the "purpose" itself.

The drive from inside is what makes the amoeba find ways to survive in new environments. It almost looks as if that amoeba would compete with other amoebas for the food supply that is present to them for this process of survival. This competition goes to such extents that members of the same species would even compete to the very end to assure their own survival.

This can be seen as subtly as the competition for survival among plants within the same garden. Or it could be as vicious as the lions fighting over territory for their hunting and roaming. Most certainly, we can see that the drive for survival is also the drive for completion or even battles. It is this completion that presses all species to find ways that provide them with tools and behaviors to assure their survival.

Perhaps we could say that it is this drive leading to competition, leading to fighting, leading to natural selection, leading to distinction of the losing side that provides the living conditions for some and elimination for others. It seems that such force is constantly within all existence to improve and to evolve. Perhaps it is not natural selection but rather a natural occurrence of change—a natural force of evolution that is not random but rather is finding the best from all that is available. Here comes the test for us to challenge our devotion and certainty in the mission the founding fathers have left us to complete. The challenge of believing in the freedom of all humanity from any subjugating force and authority that prohibits us from self-expression.

YOUR DOGMA KILLS OUR EVOLUTION

It wasn't too long ago that people believed the earth was flat and the center of the universe. As a matter of fact, people in each center of population not only believed the earth was the center of the universe, but also that their place of habitation was the sacred ground that was the center of the earth. They thought that if anybody traveled too far from their home, they would reach the end of the earth where there would be a sharp cliff, and they would fall down to oblivion; they never would be heard of or seen again. People had the belief that the sun and all the other stars were turning around the sky above the earth. This belief became so important to the humans' value system that it turned into a religious fact. The churches in the mid-tenth century had made it mandatory to believe and practice the notion that the earth was flat. Many scientists of the time had very powerful arguments why the earth was not flat. But, to say anything that would suggest the earth was not flat would be considered heresy and would bring about a horrific death sentence from the religious rulers of the time.

There was a time when spirituality and metaphysics would be considered witchcraft or a force of possession by the devil. The cure or punishment for that was to be burned in the flames of fire. There was a time when flying was considered to be a dream only to occupy foolish minds. And, along the same belief, they thought whatever went up in the sky must fall back to the ground, because the earth was the center of everything. During the sixteenth and seventeenth centuries, the Church in Europe deemed many scientists and their scientific advances heretical. The Church considered free minds, the truth-seeking scientists and the spiritual philosophers to be threats to the religious authority and well being of the societies. It's funny, but some of us still think so.

As a matter of fact, we have a "president" who is one of those funny ones. He even takes direct orders from above. Maybe he does; maybe

he doesn't. But what is important is that this type of character is not a suitable choice to be a president. I am not demeaning Mr. Bush or any other president. I believe he is aware of what he is doing and the damage he is causing. I believe, in his opinion, everything is going as planned. But whose plan is this plan, and who is going to ultimately benefit from it? I believe the plan is to derail the evolution of humanity in freedom, and Mr. Bush has designated himself as the pilot for it.

We are the people of the land where the founding fathers made plans for the next step of the evolution of humanity. We require a visionary pilot team that will take us one step further, not back, and not to destroy. We need leadership that is not influenced and infected by any dogmatic thoughts. Anything short of that is a step back toward what we all have left behind—back to the customs, traditions, and misbelieves of old.

I hope we all are clear why we live here in this country. For some, it may be the price of food, or the level of income or education, or a better standard of living. In essence, we have to understand that the first and foremost reason for our presence in this land is to keep the light of the guiding Declaration of Independence alive. This is the meaning of being an American. And many of us have forgotten that.

We have sold out to our big cars, and expensive houses, and numerous electronic toys, and our Sunday church, and the sale right before Christmas, and all-you-can-eat restaurants, and the gossip magazines. We have sold out to greed, and that greed has blinded our vision. We have forgotten why we were doing what we were doing before we got consumed.

Adams, Washington, Jefferson, Franklin, Lincoln, Kennedy are among those dedicated people in this country whose vision and leadership have taken us steps forward. Those steps were hard and expensive to take. Any damaging twist in the process damages the pace of our progress. And, surely, Mr. Bush has achieved that mission of destruction very well.

So, now let me tell you about how we got here and how this plan was put together in the shortest version possible:

(1756) Benjamin Franklin makes a new political party, attacking the ways of nonviolent Quakers, and gains massive public support. The visionary society of the Quakers, with the ideal values for humans to give each other love and nothing else, comes to an end. However, the effects of the minds and philosophy of Quakers gives the American Revolution a purpose and a direction.

(1756–1763) The Seven-Year War takes place globally between England, Spain, and France. Russia allies with France in opposition to England.

(1758–1763) The exchange of territories globally takes place between the three empires of the world. Most of these exchanges involve territories in the New World. One example is the surrender of Florida to England by Spain in exchange for getting back the Philippines on the other side of the world.

(1763–1783) The American Revolution; The Iroquois League splits apart as the union of six sovereign nations is distorted by the disagreement among its members as they struggle to decide to side with either American colonists or the English government.

(1789–1792) The French Revolution; This revolution places a directorate of five people as the head of state.

(1800) With the help of the Ottoman Empire, England puts together a new system of piracy in the Mediterranean Sea to attack all European and American merchant ships. England trains Turkish sailors in the tactics of warfare on water to attack American ships and confiscate goods. Along with such confiscations, many prisoners are sold as slaves to the harems of well-to-do Muslims.

(1801) American naval battleships are deployed on a secret mission to combat and destroy the English-supported Muslim pirate ships.

(1804) Napoleon overthrows the directorate's head of state in revolutionary France and then is crowned in the presence of the pope as yet another emperor of the great empire of France.

(1806) Despite the European embargo and the loss of America, England remains in solid opposition to the French Empire.

(1810) The population of Europe is 175 million. French Empire under the rule of Napoleon, the emperor approved by the pope, controls 50 million of this population.

(1812) Napoleon attacks Russia after Russia breaks the agreement in regard to the embargo treaty on England. Napoleon loses the war at the cost of 500,000 of his own soldiers.

(1812–1814) War of 1812 between Canada and America; The United States starts this war against Canada. The purpose of this war is to eliminate and subjugate Canada as the main ally to the sovereign nation of Native Americans. However, the war ends without a victor, and the result is a solid borderline between the two new worlds.

(1815) The empire of France begins to fall, and Napoleon is sent into exile. The Church now sees that it will need a new empire to control valuable territories. New plans are to be made. The Industrial

Revolution, a prelude to greater tools of agriculture, transportation and tools of weaponry for war is on the rise.

(1845) In America, large migration of people from Europe to the northeast United States initiates an anti-slavery movement. This movement coincides with the takeover and conquest of the Texas region from Mexico in the Mexican-American War. Since slavery had been illegal in Mexico, the new laws being practiced after Texas becomes part of the United States creates a conflict in the new balance and its territories.

(1852) Kerosene is extracted for the first time from petroleum in North America by a Canadian inventor. This changes the world of industry and the energy supply for its growth.

(1861–1865) American Civil War; The South and the North of U.S. espouse great differences in spirit and philosophy. The North brings the ideology of individualism into the social matrix whereas the South develops great estates under the system of slavery. This difference is magnified after the Texas seizure. Under Mexican rules, Texas was forbidden to practice slavery. Texas, however, overtaken by the South, is claimed for slavery. The North defeats the South and slavery becomes illegal in all regions of the U.S.

(1865) As many start-up oil companies develop in America, oil reaches a value of $20 per barrel. Rockefeller, an owner and a clerk of a shipping company who has come to a great fortune during the American Civil War, buys the first and only oil refining company. His shipping company made him money as he provided supplies to the Federal Government during the Civil War, and now his refining company supplies fuel to the growing world of industry. One of the main companies involved deeply with Rockefeller is the railroad company.

(1870) France is occupied by Germany, and Napoleon III is taken prisoner. Germany again becomes the empire of Europe. The Church initiates alliances with the German Empire.

(1873) War of Russians and Turkey Ottomans over control of territories of Serbia, Bosnia, Cyprus, and Romania begins. England and Austria oppose increased Russian influence. France breaks away from subjugation under Germany and begins to become an imperialist nation on its own once again.

(1875) Rockefeller monopolizes oil and the energy industry by force, intimidation, arms and gunmen, and influential attorneys and politicians.

(1879) Thomas Edison invents the electric lamp. Up to this point, the illumination of all streets and houses during darkness would be provided by the burning of wax candles or oil lamps and illuminating gas. This had brought a great deal of revenue to the Standard Oil Company, which monopolized the oil resources in the U.S. under the control and for the profit of Rockefeller. The invention of the electric lamp puts the oil industry at risk. However, yet another invention saves the oil industry. This invention is the internal combustion engine—automobiles. The automobile industry by Ford saves the oil industry for Rockefeller. They both realize that as long as these two industries go hand in hand, they will both profit and prosper.

(1880) Recreation of Illuminati philosophy—and then the order in Germany. This order will later become indirectly the promoter for communism, socialism, anarchism, and radicalism. Such ideologies are secondary to the real purpose of this order. This order is utilized by the German intelligence service to spread left wing ideas to neighboring countries to weaken those countries and make them easier for Germany (and, behind the scenes, the Vatican) to conquer.

(1898)The U.S. takes away Spanish territories in the western Pacific and Latin America in a war with Spain.

(1900) The Boxer Rebellion in China. This movement gained much support and strength after Japan invaded China in 1895. After that defeat, Japan and Western powers began to control and influence much of the economy and society of China. In 1900, the Chinese unite to rid the country of anyone who is not Chinese. This revolution begins with the killing of all foreigners in northern China. An international force lands in China to stop this killing rampage. China loses in the battle, and, in 1901, terms of agreement are written between the two sides. This agreement is the harshest imposed on China by Western powers. China remains dormant in the state of retaliation for the time being.

(1901) Half a million cars have been delivered to the public made by America. Standard Oil provides about one-fifth of the oil supply to the growing world. A new source of oil is found in Texas, not belonging to the Standard Oil of Rockefeller. The U.S. Supreme Court is at work breaking up Rockefeller's monopolization of the oil industry.

England as a global superpower starts losing its territories and power due to a stretched out army and navy its collapsing economy can no longer support.

(1902) Women gain the right to vote in Australia.

(1903) The Wright brothers fly the first airplane.

(1909) The Anglo-Persian Oil Company is formed. Oil is the new world commodity. England finds this commodity an avenue to regain the global power it has been losing.

China puts an end to legal slavery.

(1911) The U.S. Supreme Court breaks up Rockefeller's Standard Oil. This initiates the development of many competing oil companies.

(1914–1918) As the influence, economical strength, and wealth of European nations such as France and England increase, a preparation for gaining such powers are desired by new Germany and other nations in Europe. This is the dawn of World War I, or the "War of Imperialism. Those nations were previously under the direct control of the Church. Germany, Austria-Hungry, and Turkey become allies on one side, with Russia, France, Britain, Belgium, and Serbia on the other side joined by Japan, Italy, and the United States. Europe prepares for the war better than ever before due to technological advances of the Industrial Revolution. This is the bloodiest war so far fought among humans. Nine million die due to the power of the artillery and the planes, all fueled by petroleum. As many nations rely on petroleum as the fuel for their warfare, the U.S. gains an important place in world politics, being the largest global petroleum provider.

(1916) The Irish revolt is suppressed by England.

(1917) Russian Revolution and birth of the Soviet Union.

(1922) Mussolini takes over the government in Italy. He organizes the Fascist Party against democracy. He signs an agreement with the Vatican, and later, joins Hitler in World War II.

(1930s) Bush family, members of the secret society Skull and Bones are involved in deals with Nazi Germany. Skull and Bones is a secret society that originated from Germany and is affiliated with Illuminati. The Bush family, along with the Harrimans, Rockefellers, Nazis, neo-Nazis and leaders of the oil and pharmaceutical industries, has been instrumental in a plot to commit genetic genocide against "inferior races." Prescott Bush and George Herbert Walker are among the chief American fundraisers for the Nazi Party in the 1930s and 1940s. In return, they are rewarded with many financial opportunities from the Nazis, helping to create a great fortune and much influence among the politicians of America. This influence and connection later is utilized by the next generation of Bushes.

(1933) Hitler is appointed chancellor by Hindenburg, the president of Germany. Soon, Hitler starts political movements to convince German army and navy commanders to start a program for the conquest of "living space" for the German people.

(1933) A month after Hitler's appointment as chancellor, the German Parliament building burns down. Although the Communist party is accused as the perpetrators of the attack, evidence suggests the involvement of the Nazis. Hitler utilizes this incident for his political move as he describes the fire as the beacon from heaven. He tells reporters, "You are now witnessing the beginning of a great epoch in German history. This fire is the beginning." Soon after, a supplemental decree creates the SA (Storm Troops or Sturm Abteilung in German) and SS (Special Security) federal police agencies. This decree abrogates the following German constitutional protections in the name of national security:

- Free expression of opinion
- Freedom of press
- Right of assembly and association
- Right to the privacy of postal and electronic communication
- Protection against unlawful searches and seizures
- Individual property rights
- State's right of self-government
- Government sponsored religion based initiative.

(1934) As the Nazi party systematizes the concentration camps after it takes over all press, film industries, and the labor field. The prisoners in these camps are mostly Jews and socialists who oppose the Nazi Party. As many are executed in the name of national security, the German people allow this reign of terror to take control of the entire nation without any significant resistance or expression of outrage, for they believe this is going to bring power and unity back to their nation. Germany develops the best-known modern example of a government-sponsored religious-based initiative as Nazi Germany. The conflict between England and Germany is on the issue of the existence and involvement of the Jewish population in the world domination plans. I do not want to go into details with this subject, as the English royal family's long history of cultural and genome connections to the Jewish population of Briton may create more complexity at this point.

(1941) America enters WWII as a superpower with its own large supply of petroleum.

(1945) After American victory and the fall of the Nazi regime in mainland Europe, many German officers, advisors to Adolph Hitler, are brought to America to serve in the new American secret intelligence agency, later becoming CIA. They are known for their clever skills and ruthless planning to achieve results. They are also well known for their internal knowledge of the system of socialism and communism that Germans had designed and injected into Russia.

(1960) America's addiction to oil demands a greater need for petroleum. However, the domestic supply of petroleum does not seem to be at sufficient levels any longer. England enters the American market. Since England does not have any petroleum resources of its own, it finds other undeveloped nations to subjugate to access the highly demanded fuel supply of the West.

(1963) John F. Kennedy is assassinated.

(1967) Robert F. Kennedy promises "change and hope" for a struggling society under the burden of the Vietnam War and doubt. As he also is assassinated, youths and minorities find themselves within such intensity only short of the force of the civil war raised a hundred years prior. The country is on the verge of division.

George H.W. Bush who has already experienced a great success in the Republican Party politics is now experiencing a defeat as running for the U.S. Senate.

(1971–1976) George H. Walker. Bush is selected for a series of high-profile appointments: Ambassador to the United Nations in 1971, Chairman of the Republican National Committee in 1973, envoy to china in 1974, and finally the position of the director of CIA in 1976. By now, Bush is heavily involved in the business of crude oil, and has made substantial amount of profit. Since Bush is involved in the industry of oil, his political involvement with good old friends such as Rockefellers and the Saudi royal family, who are all involved in the acquisition of the most valuable commodity of the time, crude oil seems most profitable.

Bush loses his position as the director of CIA once Jimmy Carter was elected President in 1976. Bush has no other place but to return to private life. However, in 1980 to the surprise of many Republicans, Ronald Reagan selects bush as his running mate for the White House. The Bush family climbs the ladder of power to continue a century-long plan.

During the period of time when George H.W. Bush was appointed as the director of CIA, plans for a mock terrorist attack on a hundred-story building were put in place.

The head of 1976 mock terrorist plan, Lt. Michael Teague of Long Island, given specific orders from unknown superiors to use the Twin Towers as terrorist targets. Such plans indicate very similar exploit of the passenger airline carriers flown by terrorist pilots into the Twin Towers later used in 2001. (Please refer to Timothy McNiven's lawsuit. McNiven was a U.S. Defense Department

Operative who was still under contract with government in 2005, and has been revealing many documents claiming the involvement of Bush with the 911. He even took a lie detector test to prove his documents were real, which he passed.)

(2000) Bush is declared president by the U.S. Supreme Court after massive election fraud perpetrated by his brother, the governor of the state of Florida. Soon, Bush pushes tax cuts for the wealthy through Congress, and commands the FBI to stop investigations concerning the Bin Laden family and other suspected terrorist cells.

(2001) Sept. 11, the World Trade Center and the Pentagon come under attack. The organization of the hijackers has close financial ties with the Bush family. As the American public grows suspicious in the matters of the Bush administration involvement with this act of terrorism, Bush forces the USA Patriot Act through Congress. This bill suspends many essential civil liberties, justifying repression as vital to the "war on terrorism." The act of questioning this authority and disagreement is considered treason. Despite the Posse Comitatus Act of 1878, which was placed into effect after the civil war to limit powers of federal government to use military for law enforcement over non-federal properties and civilians, a presidential decree makes it possible for military forces to be used to monitor the public. Soon after, a supplemental decree gives authority to the National Security Agency (NSA) to overstep the constitutional rights of the American people. The Patriot Act abrogates the following American constitutional protections:

- Free expression of opinion
- Freedom of press
- Right of assembly and association
- Right to privacy of postal and electronic communications
- Protection against unlawful searches and seizures
- Individual property rights
- State's right of self-government
- Government-sponsored, religion-based initiatives

If you have paid close attention, it is apparent that the Roman Catholic Church has always been a support for the existence of an empire under its supervision to control vast areas of the world throughout history. A religious restriction follows such subjugation for all people under the empire. England is obviously the other side of the coin to this equation. It, too, wants world domination under its system of imperialism, a system competing back-to-back with the Vatican empire. And, as we know, when two things are back to back, their survival remains sustained for as long as the existence of the other backing is assured. The two sides need each other. Nevertheless, they are at war.

The war is over the control of the land of the United States and its people, and the opponents are, on one side, the good old Vatican, and on the other side, the great empire of England, land of Angles, the people who planned the construction of the New World, under the direction and guidance of the English imperial kingdom. For the time being, today, the two opponents can join momentarily when they have a common obstacle to overcome; the obstacle to overcome is the very price of the battle itself, and that is the U.S.A.

LOCATION, LOCATION, LOCATION...

In 1960, the nations forming OPEC, most of the Arab nations, achieved a memorable victory in the progress of their union. They initiated a move that was well planned for the following thirty-five years, and the move started at the time by accepting the kingdom of Iran as a member. Historically, the Arabs had never accepted Iranians into their crowds and societies. Arabs always called the Iranians "Ajam." "Ajam" in Arabic means the outsider or whoever is not an Arab but lives in proximity to Arabs. In particular, according to Arab nations, Iranians are "Ajam" because they practice a distorted version of Islam that called "Shiite." The Arabs always had kept in mind that the best use of Iranians, or Shiites, was to subjugate them under slavery. But in 1960, they accepted Iran, a Shiite country, to be a great part of OPEC. So why such sudden change of heart to give important access to Iran?

The answer will reveal itself as we review what happened in that area for the following thirty years. However, before we focus only on what was happening at that time in the Middle East, we also need to understand that one of the first five countries organizing OPEC along with Iraq, Iran, Kuwait, and Saudi Arabia was the faraway country of Venezuela. And there also are Arab countries that are *not* members of OPEC, such as Oman and Syria. Our review will clarify the complexity of the events that concluded in such an arrangement. We'll start with the events of December 1973, when, all of a sudden lines of cars piled up at gas stations all over the U.S. The lineup was a result of the embargo the Arabic countries had imposed on the U.S. as the war between the Arabs and Israel erupted earlier that year.

During this embargo, although the shah of Iran raised the price of oil dramatically, he remained an ally to the U.S. by not only providing oil to the West but also allowing American ships to dock and fuel at Iranian harbors. This act was the ignition for the plan the Arabs hatched for the removal of the shah from their proximity. Obviously, the shah did not appear to be a reliable player in the long-term plan

for attack and terrorism and the final destruction of America. Nevertheless, the embargo against America was lifted nearly a year later by
the Arabs. The risky move started by the war that was initiated
against Israel a year earlier now earned great rewards—it brought the
Arabs financial bounty. One of those rewards was an enormous
increase in the annual revenue from oil. Saudi Arabia's rose from $4
billion to $36 billion a year. Iraq's rose from $2 billion to $9 billion,
and Kuwait's rose from $2 billion to $9 billion. Where did the money
go? Nowhere but to the construction of armies, over- and under-
ground, in those Middle East countries.

In 1978, when the export of the oil from Iran was halted due to the
Shiite movement of Iranians against the rule of shah, the price of oil
exported from Arabic countries jumped up another 150 percent. You
need to realize that Iran historically has been providing only 5 percent
of the oil to the international community. As a matter of fact, OPEC
altogether has provided only 40 percent of the oil production for the
globe. So, a jump in the price of oil by such a great rate that OPEC
was claiming from the world would not seem acceptable at first look.
However, the members of OPEC held 77 percent of the oil reserve in
the world. So, obviously, any move made by the OPEC countries to
change the price of oil has great leverage and will take a great toll on
the non-OPEC oil producing countries.

This is the threat that the countries in OPEC hold against the rest of
the world. Arabs had wanted to gain vast global control for hundreds
of years. The battle between them and the U.S. had long been
announced as a jihad that many Muslims would soon be ready for and
clearly act upon its demands. But the only factor that remained as an
obstacle to this control was the penetration of America through Iran
in the center of the Middle East. And as long as the friendship and
support of the shah of Iran by the U.S. remained intact, a stranger—
or, better said, a trader in the eyes of the Arabs—would be present to
disturb the union and planning of the Arab thoughts and ideology. So,
only did this support somehow need to be severed, but also the remnants of the base of the U.S. Army had to be cleaned out of the area.
That is when the ego-saturated shah of Iran was encouraged by the
deceitful Arabic oil producing nations to challenge America to gain
financial independence for the people of Iran. It was commonly com-
municated by the people of the Middle East that the shah of Iran was
America's policeman in the area. This bothered the shah, and consequently he changed the history of the world with an unwise decision.

Up until this point, the United States had relied on its relationship with the shah of Iran, especially since the embargo of 1973, and Iran had remained an ally to the West. However, at a particularly sensitive and pivotal moment in the history of humanity, the shah of Iran cut his vitally important close ties with America. The shah's vision was to bring the newly revived country of Iran to the table of the big players in world politics. And, for that, he believed that the Persian Empire once again would have the power it had achieved 2,500 years ago. Or, perhaps, he received misleading information from the authorities and the directors of the CIA.

I remember the night when I was twelve years old, watching TV as my parents were having a conversation with several guests they had over for dinner. On the TV, the shah gave his national speech and announced that a great opportunity had arisen for the Iranians that would place them right at, and then beyond, the "gates of civilization." He asked Iranians to remain at his side to reach those golden gates together. He obviously had recognized the fact that Iranians had missed the turn that separated the civilized and uncivilized worlds long ago. But now he believed was the time to make a radical move to bring the people of Iran to the missed gates and give them access to a new world—a world of honor and respect.

He talked about Western civilization concurrently as he renounced having ineffective ties with the West when Iran would have profited more from such ties. He announced that the price of oil would be nearly doubled if such ties were to remain intact. I remember his speech, and I remember thinking to myself, "I think the world has just changed forever..." At the time, I did not know how the world shook after such speech. But now, many years later, I realize that this moment must have been the turning point. The beginning of the inclination of the wave of the war, which we will come to see in America in the near future, had just been initiated. It was done unintentionally by the premature speech of a visionary ruler of a troubled part of the world. The shah had lost his connection with the very source that had kept him alive all along.

It was a night when a long-time ally and friend had severed his bond with the U.S. and had cut ties in regard to the supply of oil to the West—the shah had announced that the price of oil must be increased dramatically and immediately if the Western nations remained interested in utilizing it for their livelihood. You might remember or have read about the fear that took over the lives of people in the U.S. when the news was given about that speech. That speech almost started a second oil crisis, one similar to the struggle for its industrial life that the U.S. went through the first time in 1973. So, why did a long-time ally turn so dramatically and suddenly to cut all ties and reliance the West had come to trust and depend upon—especially with the threat of the USSR invading Afghanistan?

Clearly, the U.S. made a horrible mistake to let such disconnection take place. Not only did it not realize the presence of the trap that was had been laid, but the U.S. also indirectly helped remove the shah through President Jimmy Carter, who reprimanded the shah for his inhumane treatment of a captured and imprisoned terrorist. Not so long after this disconnection, a long-term cleric, an enemy of the shah who had remained dormant in exile, rose and started a move against the shah and his government. The plan of the Arab nation had now entered the second stage—the removal of the shah, the obstacle to the movement of the Islamic nation to gain union and strength to fight the long enemy of Islam, the infidel nation of America. The key player to this next move was already there brewing for many years. His name was Khomeini, who was first placed in Najaf, Iraq, and then had moved to France. The chess game was taking shape exactly as the Muslim nations wanted. And the U.S. remained apathetically clueless.

The next moves the Muslims made in this chess game were simple. Nevertheless, those critical moves remained to be illusive to the eyes of the Western nations, especially the Unites States, which were busy reaching higher levels of mental and physical evolution of self-expression and self-acknowledgment—a fragile state of mind in meditation that could be taken advantage of by the outside hostile forces as one becomes unconscious of what is around. And that is exactly what happened to the people in the U.S. They were taken by surprise as the shah fell and Khomeini, with the help of the Islamic terrorists, gained control of the cleric-oriented minds of Iranians. The crazed people of Iran soon attacked the American Embassy, taking the American diplomats hostage, a move that no one had dared to even think of for centuries under international policies.

The occupation of the American Embassy in Tehran without retaliation from the U.S. was a portrayal of Khomeini's power within his movement through the clerics of Iran. As he acknowledged his victory, Khomeini expressed to the neighboring Arabic countries his desire to gain more control of the Middle East area. His announcement of his intentions to "export Islam to the infidel world" was ignored by the Western countries. Nevertheless, his first move in his demand was to take control of the Shiite world. This demand was not in concurrence with what was discussed between Arabs and the team of Khomeini prior to the ignition of plans to remove the shah. Arabs now found themselves facing an anticipated challenge they had dreaded prior to the takeover of Khomeini in Iran. However, there had all along been a means of isolation between the Sunni Muslim Arabic countries and the non-controllable Shiite Muslim country of Iran. A neighboring tyrant who had shown his abilities to viciously and carelessly attack his opponents seemed to be a solution for confrontation with the new peeve in Iran. There was no better choice for Arabs but to have an internal war within the Middle East against Khomeini and his movement, led by such a neighboring tyrant. This tyrant was no one else but the infamous Saddam, and there was no better person for this attack but Saddam, to do what he wanted to do for many years. After all, since Saddam himself was a possible threat to the plans of the Arabs to create an Islamic movement through terrorism, any harm sent his way would not be a loss to the Arab countries and their

Islamic focus. He was dispensable in the eyes of Arabic Muslim who could be used as a future distraction tool while the Muslim countries would prepare for war against America.

Saddam was an Arabic nationalist whose desires always were to unite and expand the Arabic nations under his vision and ruling. This vision had always been a conflict with the religious oriented politics of the Muslim countries. Muslim politicians did not consider Saddam a part of their team and its plan. As a matter of fact, Muslims had plans to remove Saddam from his ruling authority in Iraq; after all, Saddam did not share the same vision to fight the West by acts of terrorism. He desired to be the "cowboy" of the Middle East who would use his mighty power to combat the great forces of "the West." And he wanted to prove his worthiness to the rest of the Arab people by invading Iran, an outsider country that remained a substantial peeve in the eyes of the Middle East.

Saddam attacked Iran with no consequences or scolding for his inhumane war tactics from any other neighboring countries or others around the world. He was given cover as he used chemical and biological warheads to combat the army of Khomeini and his new conformation. In some instances, even Russia helped provide goods for Saddam's air force against Iran for what Iran's Hezbollah had done to the Russian army in Afghanistan. But Khomeini remained determined in what he wanted to achieve, even at the cost of hundreds of thousands of young soldiers who were devoted to him and his vision. Nothing mattered to Khomeini but retaliation and incursion of Iraq first, then moving on into Israel and eliminating it from the Middle East, and then finding ways to combat the U.S.

Khomeini had a vision to create an Islamic gathering, a wave of events, and expansion of Islamic governments to neighboring countries and eventually to the world with a passion to destroy America. As Khomeini continued to fight back and not give up any land or power, Arabs realized they were losing focus on the main vision for the chess game they had in mind, which was to defeat the Western infidels. They realized they had to accept that perhaps Iranians were the hidden key they had long been missing in the war with America. This brought Iranians and Arabs to a new level of understanding, a new agreement that became imminent in many events that brought us to an awakening tragedy on a Tuesday morning we all now know as 9/11. It was an announcement that Saudi Arabia and Iran and their compilation of powers and connections made to the world for the position they now held in the international community. A threat had just shown its ugly head. A warning that once was ignored by the rest of the world was now beginning to show its face to the unattended globe. And the monstrous body would follow. But how did it all get to this point?

We are all familiar with the hunt for Osama Bin Laden for his connections to the 9/11 terrorist attack on the Twin Towers in New York City. However, what we pay least attention to is the connections Bin Laden had with the government of the U.S. in the mid-to-late-1980s. During that decade, the Soviet Union had penetrated into Afghanistan to gain control and closer access to free waters. It was an act of expansion by the struggling government of the USSR to secure its own existence. It was the last attempt the USSR would make prior to the loss of the control it had gained after more than sixty years of continuous growth in the region against the United States. But, if we look deeper into this clandestine circle of events, we find close encounters of the newly developing terrorist groups of Hezbollah from Iran and the CIA in training a small group of Sunni fighters who migrated from Saudi Arabia to Afghanistan to fight against Russia. Although Iran remained hostile toward the U.S., it seemed that a common enemy would be justification for the U.S. to join and train the seemingly less powerful enemy, the lesser of two evils. BIG MISTAKE. Or perhaps the directors of CIA had other plans.

The Soviet Union was defeated and pushed out of Afghanistan just prior to the middle of the 1980s with the fighters of Hezbollah and al Qaeda giving guidance to the Afghani fighters. After removal of Soviet control over Afghanistan, a new group of tyrants subjugated the Afghani people. The Taliban took over the abandoned and vulnerable country of Afghanistan—a country struggling with a sick infrastructure that had been arbitrarily run by the barbarians of the area for thousands of years, a perfect place for the growth of yet another organized criminal barbaric ideology that now had plans to expand and inject its own infection into the rest of the world, an infected ideology that we have come to know as Islam, a violent subjugation that defies any level of harmony with the rest of the world with different views of life. The rest of the world is what Islam calls the "infidels," and an infidel is subject to execution if it resists accepting Islam. But why is it that the civilized world was so blinded to such dangerous Islamic movements in the recently financially independent Middle East countries? Why didn't we pay more attention to a plan that has always been elucidated so openly among Islamic countrymen?

There is an explanation for such OVERLOOK on our part, but first let's go back to when Iraq and Iran were in the final stages of their war. In the late 1980s, Saddam had reached levels of usage of chemical and biological warheads beyond what could be hidden from the world. The U.S. then injected itself into the war by investigating and perhaps aiding Iraq in ways to defeat Iran without using such weapons. Nevertheless, as all politicians can fall into the trap of corruption, the investigation of Saddam by the U.S. Army fell into heavy traps of such bribery, a bribe that was given from the Arabs to the investigators to let the games move forward. Although the acceptance of bribery might not have seemed to be harmful to the U.S. at the time, the effects of that acceptance snowballed and the question challenged the integrity of the U.S. Army for many years to come.

The chess game then encountered an unexpected move, one not calculated by the U.S. as a consequence of the wrong decisions the American inspectors made to keep their integrity. Some of the well-known inspectors of that event became important team members of Bush in the year 2000, which brought us to the wave of conflicts that are coming our way. The question on everyone's mind on that Tuesday of September 11 was: How could we be so fragile and affected by the actions of a radical all the way on the other side of the world, and why in hell did we have any connections to a dictator who was known to torture his own people just for pleasure? Or was it that Saddam was controlling the wave of the terrorism by creating fear in the area, and we just did not understand this valuable obstacle that was inhibiting the growth of terrorism in the area. And that is when the anti-American side of the chess game gained control of the game.

Arabs knew what to do not only to get rid of this obstacle to what they wanted to achieve—that is, to create unity for the grounds for the terrorists to roam on—but also bring the forces of America closer to a battlefield they could fight on more easily. This was the plan:

They make a deal with Iran to join forces in their war against America. As Iran accepted the offer Saudis extended to them, Khomeini—seemingly unhappy—appeared to announce giving up to the terms of Saddam Hussein. Saddam was convinced to return to Iraq, for the time being, without any gain of land from Iran but was promised to gain oil and money by taking over Kuwait. This was a plan Arabs held to use Saddam for future bait for the U.S. Saudis included Iran in their master plan and forged close ties in their common focus on their enemy, the United States. Iran had gained respect for its solid anti-American behavior that contained no fear of the consequences of their disrespect to all international laws. As a matter of fact, Iran defied the strength of the U.S. and the powerful image it had gained in the international community.

Saudi Arabia and Iran become the queen and king of the chess game. Iran moved forward with its plans to construct nuclear capabilities and warheads that could carry such weapons far distances. But Saudis and Iranians knew the U.S. was about to attack them. They needed a scapegoat quickly and effectively. They then needed to utilize Saddam for what he was intended to be used for all the time. They invest in a presidential campaign that surely would bring them to a safer zone for this attack. The elected president, with much financial support from the Arabs, has a friendship with them and an animosity against Saddam. So they create 9/11 to deter the attention of the plan of attack of the U.S. from a global level to a limited army combat in Afghanistan and then later to Iraq. They use Saddam by encouraging him to once again stand in front of the world announcing that he possesses great power and does not need the U.S. because he has weapons of mass destruction (WMD). Saddam falls for the trick and gives the go-ahead for war with U.S., thinking Iran and Saudi Arabia will support him in the war. He is used for the next move to lure the U.S. into a battle where the U.S. would lose if its soldiers were to remain there. Now, America cannot attack any more countries. The main powers behind the enemy of the U.S. remain unharmed and strong. Iran, North Korea, and Saudi Arabia remain in control of this game. The question now is: Can we get out of this losing game?

First, we need to understand who is behind the master plan by which the Muslim terrorists in and out of the Middle East are guided. Do you remember the days when the army of the U.S. in Iraq was fighting insurgents, many of whom were entering from Iran? And did you know that Prince Charles went to visit the authorities in Tehran during the early days of 2004? To be exact: February 9, 2004. The secret meeting was covered up under the pretext of his consideration for the earthquake that happened the previous December in Bam. Perhaps there are many other events and connections that are happening in Iran that we are not paying enough attention to.

Muslims need land. They need ground for expansion of population, strength, and influence, and construction of their plans. They will do what it takes to slowly but surely gain access and penetration into different societies all around the world. They will behave as wolves in sheepskins until they are close to the target. Their goal is to claim what their prophecy has promised them for more than a thousand years—to rule and control the world under Allah and to purify the earth from all infidelities the natural human mind has suffered from. Their goal is to cover up any behaviors in humanity that will open to question the nature of our evolution. Under Islam, there is only one way to live and to let live, and that is the way of Islam, a repressive ideology that has no respect for any of the human rights that are the main amendments in the American Constitution. For that reason, the American Constitution is what the Koran, the holy book of Islam, calls the words of evil. Muslims will try forever to destroy America and its Constitution because it is their devout responsibility to obliterate what they see as the evil confronting them.

Conversely, we also need to remember the conflicts that have existed between the Fatimids, or the Shiites, and the Caliphates, or the Sunnis. Perhaps a clandestine plan exists where the Shiites finally have found a solution to destroy their disagreeable teammates—actually competition—by involving them in a war with "infidels" they do not care for. Their goal is what they anticipate to be the outcome: the weakness and destruction of both enemies by each other. The Persian Empire has found a new state doctrine to unite under.

The wave is coming, and it will not be easy for us to survive it. But we need to prepare for it. The pirates of the Middle East under the English flag have gained control, and they are about to land on our shores. We need to be ready for the war that is coming closer to us. We need to be ready to surpass the wave of hostility that is coming our way. We need to evaluate our thoughts, beliefs, and understanding of the Constitution of the Unites States. And we need to keep in mind that we need to assert our right to have guns for when it is time to confront those who try to destroy this Constitution.

I salute the men and women of integrity who are serving our country, our ideology, protecting it as they put their lives in danger. I salute all the soldiers whose care and sense of dignity are taking us forward during difficult times as such.

I also urge a trial of the mobs that have taken over our country ripping it apart for their own greed and hunger for power. I urge the people of America to unite and bring to court a false central government that is taking the lives of our soldiers and citizens in vain.

Terrorist attacks may or will take place. What could be the most destructive effects of a terrorist attack is how we may restrict our own personal civil rights as a result. What we need to prepare for is how we are going to respond to such attacks without eroding our own values and civil liberties.

TAGHIEH

(Prevarication) = (Parthian Shot)

We were watching the news on TV tonight about the war in Iraq. The newscaster was giving information about a horrible act of an Arabic terrorist group that had unjustifiably beheaded someone who happened to be from where else but the United States. The group had announced that this act of punishment was in revenge for what had happened in the prisons of Iraq, for what the prisoners had gone through with nudity and so forth. This act was totally unexplainable for the fact that the terrorist group did not need an excuse to do what they had done in the first place.

What the Arab terrorist group was claiming by this act was that they would only retaliate when Americans did something wrong. So, they made an effort to show to the world that there is a reason for what they do, which is terrorizing and killing those who cannot defend themselves, to achieve receiving what they want. And that is what a terrorist is. A terrorist is one who forces his/her desires and wishes by creating threats to make others find no other way out but what is given to them by the enforcer. Terrorists get away with this forceful control, because most people find the alternative to what may happen to them even more fearful. So, they are saying that whenever there is injustice by anyone in the world against the Arabs, the partic-ular group would pay back and punish the guilty by beheading a member of the guilty society. Pretty much like the Mafia and how they punish their unfavorable threats.

There is something very fundamentally wrong about this behavior. First of all, punishment of a member of a guilty group who has not been proven to be guilty will not create growth and evolution of our minds. Rather, it creates a sense of fear and disharmony that disables all who are involved in such environments. Second, even if one is found to be guilty of a crime, that does not mean he or she needs to be punished by death. A guilty party needs to be given a chance, an instrument to correct the mistake and make up for what happened that was wrong. But you do not find a healthy set of rules in such practices as the Mafia or Islam.

Later on, during the same TV program, there was an interview with a professor who was originally Arabic himself and has been known to be an authority in describing the minds of the Arab world. He was asked about this behavior and what had happened. He was asked how Arab societies would respond to such acts. He explained in detail how this act is so rejected and would create a feeling of disgust among the Arab people. I was amazed by what he was saying. He knew he was lying through his teeth; nevertheless, he was giving such passionate testimony that Arab societies would oppose such acts. He explained how the Arabs do not like to be exposed to such acts of violence. And he is a professor who talks and acts very American; therefore, people in our society give him credibility.

The truth remains different than what he was presenting. Those Arab societies have been infected by such behaviors and rules for hundreds of years. They have public lashings, hangings, stoning, and different types of executions in front of an audience on the streets in Saudi Arabia, Iran, Iraq, Pakistan, and all the other Muslim countries where they have a chance to behave in the utmost accurate Islamic rulings. If such acts are not observed in the daily news on our TV channels, it does not mean that people in that area are not practicing or accepting such behavior. The truth is that those people infected by Islam would not find it fundamentally wrong to behead someone or kill them by stoning if such act takes place for the purposes of their religious beliefs. So why is it that the professor was lying through his teeth and who was he trying to protect?

It is written in the Koran that if your life as a Muslim is in danger because of "righteous" actions you took, it is approved if you would hide your true intentions and pretend to be someone else rather than whom you really are. In short, first you have to fight anybody and any philosophy or religion that does not accept the teachings of Moham- mad to be accurate and true. Second, these infidels must be con- fronted, and if they do not get quiet or discontinue their disbelief, they must be killed. Third, if this action causes problems for the involved Muslims, for instance, if the infidels are too powerful and have taken over, the Muslims can hide their true beliefs and pretend to be sorry about what they did. Once the situation is safe again, they can con- tinue their duties as a Muslim. This act is called "taghieh."

If the basis of trust in the world would be to do what one says and to say what one thinks, then Muslims could not be trusted. The religion of Islam strictly demands harsh action toward those who disbelieve their way of thinking, and, if the circumstances are too difficult for their true beliefs, they can pretend to be someone they are not until they have the chance to overcome what is separate from them.

England appears to be an ally of America. It appears to have joined us in the war against terrorism. But we cannot ignore the bitterness England has kept against America ever since the Declaration of Independence was written by Thomas Jefferson, which concluded in England's loss of power over a lucrative colony the English always have thought to be theirs. We cannot forget the fact that England supported and encouraged the Muslim pirates when the American naval ships were on a mission to destroy such infection. And we must be reminded that this mission was started by Thomas Jefferson, the author of the Declaration of Independence that brought a war upon the English empire. England has not forgotten such loss and will continue its clandestine plans until America caves in.

I was speaking with an intelligent, middle-aged American who seemed very curious about my opinion on the subject we just talked about in this chapter. After the conclusion I made in regards to the wave that is coming our way, he mentioned that he has had his sixty-foot yacht prepared with necessities for survival to travel down south and far away from the commotion if a war takes place in our homeland. I was very surprised and saddened to hear what he had to say. And I replied, "I would stay because I believe we would need to protect the Constitution of the United States." The answer he gave me was the typical denial we have been seeing in our society. He said, "It is easier to stay away from the danger and let the war take its course and then return to rebuild and reinstate the rule of the Constitution. Meanwhile, we could watch that war on CNN!"

But the world is not flat, my friend. The planet is only so large, or, actually, so small. We have migrated for tens of thousands of years from the Stone Age to modern humanity. We have constantly been walking away from the problems we had encountered in our residing environment without resolving them. But now, we are reaching the boundaries of a migration that soon will place us back to where we started from in the first place—because the world, my friends, is not flat. The world is round and no matter which direction you go, you will find previous troubled and left-behind grounds in the future. But you have to find one important answer to the cause of wars on earth and in the Middle East. What is the reason that the Jewish people have been targeted for thousands of years by all others in Europe and the Middle East? What is the truth that has been kept from us that has not been paid attention to? I will share this truth with you, and I hope this will be a start to take a good look at our behaviors, and ourselves and once and for all put behind us the primitive behaviors that have haunted us throughout the long years of ice ages.

But one thing remains an issue that we need to recognize throughout the history of humankind. Many humans have migrated, hoping for a new land, a new world in which they can be far and away from all troubles they left behind. Cro-Magnons left Africa and migrated to

Europe; Aryans migrated to India, Asia Minor, and northern Europe; Celts migrated away from Romans into Britain; and Brits and other Europeans, along with many others from all over the world, migrated to the New World, the Americas. All those migrations were done to leave behind the troubles that were bothering us somewhere we lived before. We left, but the problems stayed. The problems stayed, and they manifested and grew larger. As those problems grow, they reach proximity to wherever we live now. Perhaps we might want to continue walking away. And guess what? The world is not flat. If we continue to walk away from what is chasing us, we will end up at the same place we once left behind.

Wars over fire, vegetables, and the bridge connecting east to west will continue to the end of time for humanity. We have to change the nature of this war fundamentally or it will reach and consume us. We as humans have to see the big picture before we destroy ourselves. The world needs leadership to make such great change. That leadership must come from the most advanced society of humanity, a society that has brought a compilation of the greatest brains on earth. That society is the United States of America. We have the responsibility— because we are Americans.

FREEDOM FOR EVERYONE BUT THE ENEMIES OF FREEDOM

Every living being, including every human, has the same right to freedom regardless of their color, beliefs, preference in the way of living, race, gender, and their species' position in the tree of life—up to the point where their actions would interfere with the privacy, freedom, and well-being of others in such a tree. Understanding such notions will provide the preservation of this freedom. By securing such universal understanding among all living beings, religious, racial, and cultural, prioritizing becomes trivial and ineffective. In actuality, belief in any nationalistic, religious, and credulous traditions whereby a specific group claims to be "the chosen one" is an action against universal respect for the rights of freedom for all others living within nature.

Have you ever noticed when it is that you are the happiest? Keep track of what you do on a daily basis. Also, keep track of your moods and emotions during the same times. Compare and make note of when you are the happiest and you will find that you are the happiest when you find the freedom to do what you want to do. Whatever it is that makes you truly happy has to do with a sense of freedom you feel. That sense of freedom could be for a selfish matter or could be for giving. Nevertheless, when we feel we have the freedom to do what we want to do, we become ecstatic and energetic. We become happy. It also is undeniable that our happiness multiplies as the happiness of the others around us increases as well. Look at how much fun everyone has in a public park or amusement park or how we like to dance in a club full of people rather than the vacant living room in our own house. What I am trying to make clear here is that when we are truly happy, we want others around us also to be truly happy, even if it is for our own selfish reasons. Happiness of others increases our own happiness. And the way we can provide happiness for the masses is to secure an environment where freedom and privacy of all is respected.

It is a natural law to seek happiness, because happiness is the key to maintaining freedom.

Some people misunderstand the important yet delicate fact about freedom, and say that if everyone is free to do what he or she would like to do, then how could it be wrong if someone decides to utilize his or her freedom to control others? If you are asking the same question, I urge you to repeat the question out loud to yourself and then just think about it for a few more moments. I am certain that once you do so, you will realize the problem that activating such a statement would bring upon us. It is imperative to maintain an environment that would sustain the state of freedom for all living beings contained within this web of life. There is a role for each member of this web of life as we see it, and that role can only be enhanced when the characters of the web of life have the freedom to express themselves fully and in freedom.

There is a purpose to everything that is a part of our lives. Everything within the system of our bodies, the system of our natural food chain, and the system of the characteristics of the physical formation has a purpose, a reason to be there. Throughout our evolutions, many characteristics that did not have any role, or had unfavorable effects, were eliminated by nature and its power of selection—a selection for the survival of the characteristics that had the role in the web of life that was being formed to create harmony among all the members of such web. Nature eliminates those and their characteristics that do not have a favorable role, an effect, and a purpose in the web of life. Most definitely, nature will eliminate those who have such unfavorable effects on the well-being of the very "web of life" that is in the progress of evolving. Anything, any belief, or anybody who would disturb this environment will be eliminated from our globe. This elimination is done by nature via many avenues, including wars that we humans initiate. Fighting is constructive only if it delivers liberty and justice for all.

Thinking and focusing in an alarmist manner is a destructive behavior that can take away the key state of mind of happiness. Keeping a society under the effects of an alarmist state of mind creates a broad panic that ultimately weakens and possibly disassembles it. We fail to evolve in our web of life as a society when we focus on aspects of fear and sorrow. Let me make a simple example to clarify the effects of an alarmist behavior. Have you ever been around someone who always talks fearfully of getting sick—like someone in your family or among your friends who is always afraid of catching flu? I am sure if you look around for a while, you might find someone with such an attitude.

Think of someone who is so concerned and worried about, for instance, getting sick even from a little cold wind, and who articulates that fear every time we are around him or her. Sometimes, such people extend their fears out of their love for us, to warn us. They would alarm us about the chances of catching a cold every time we walk outside after a shower, or getting sick from a wind, however pleasant it could be, or what might happen to us if we walk barefoot on the cold floor, or what might happen to us if we eat certain types of food. This fear can be very destructive and counterproductive.

Once someone develops such fear-based beliefs, they set up a defense mechanism in the brain. The brain is the executive organ within our bodies by which other functional organs receive messages in harmony with their role. So, whatever message we develop within our brains will become the truth that exists in our perception of life around us. If we believe that a pleasant cool breeze can make us sick, then every fresh draft that touches the face or body sends a defense mechanism to the entire body. The immune system becomes active and the "reactive reserves" are utilized to prepare the body against external factors. In people with such defensive mentality, this whole reaction of body against the smallest stimulants can become habitual. Such habitual defense mechanisms can become degenerative in two ways:

First, hyperactivity of amygdalae hippocampus, a part of Limbic system responsible to perform a primary role in the processing and memory of emotional reactions. Hyperactivity of this complex organ causes atrophy of this Limbic system. At the very least, this causes behaviors that are a prelude to isolation—progressive decline of higher cognitive function, memory, attention, planning, language—that all affect the understanding and the improvement of better standards of living by the one suffering.

The next page illustrates the cycle of events taking place to raise a specific reaction from us in any given circumstance. What we do reply to a given state is how the components of our brains have been conditioned and trained to function; to act or react. And the result is what makes our lives different from one another. The Cycle of events starts from the top left side of the page;

"Role of Circle of relations by Amygdalae"
"State of mind = quality of life"

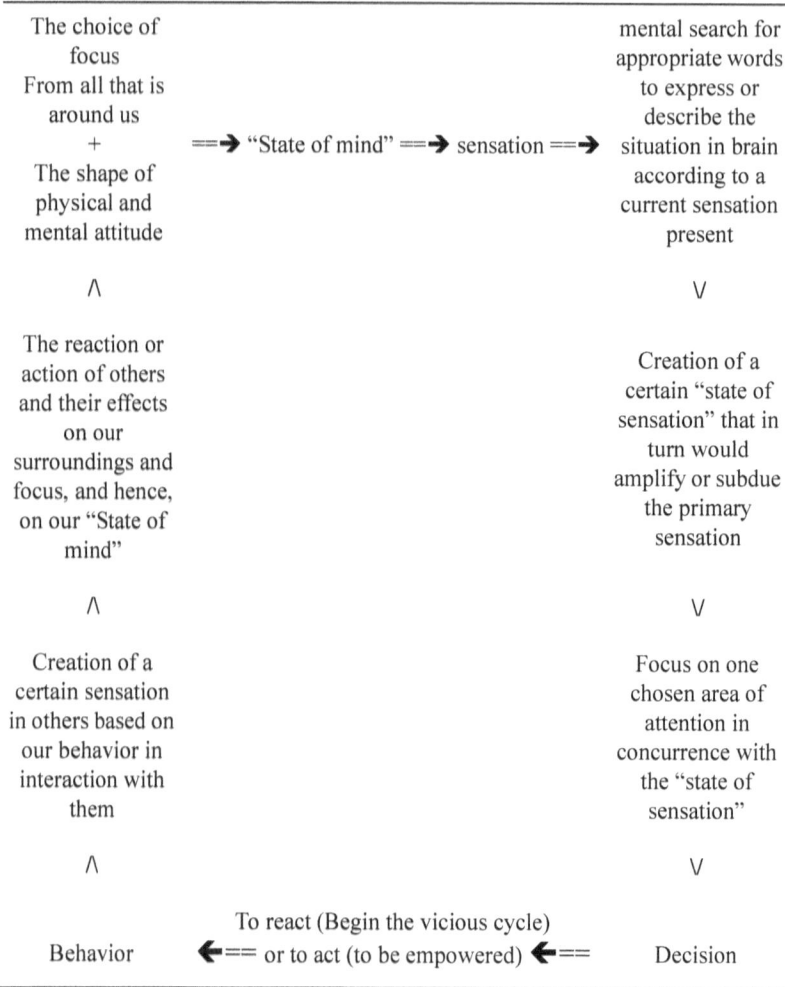

The choice of focus From all that is around us + The shape of physical and mental attitude

==➔ "State of mind" ==➔ sensation ==➔

mental search for appropriate words to express or describe the situation in brain according to a current sensation present

∧

∨

The reaction or action of others and their effects on our surroundings and focus, and hence, on our "State of mind"

Creation of a certain "state of sensation" that in turn would amplify or subdue the primary sensation

∧

∨

Creation of a certain sensation in others based on our behavior in interaction with them

Focus on one chosen area of attention in concurrence with the "state of sensation"

∧

∨

To react (Begin the vicious cycle)

Behavior   ⬅== or to act (to be empowered) ⬅==   Decision

This equation illustrates how our psychology of reaction to our environment creates the world we individually live in. This continuous cycle starts from the top left of the page, and it continues to feed itself as it returns to the same point after the digestion of the emotions one goes through. Basically, the meanings we give to what is going on around us will shape our lives continuously.

Second, the body soon becomes depleted from the "reactive reserves" so that when there is a true and massive attack of a harmful substance, the body is simply too tired to fight back.

So, please do not misunderstand what I am about to say, because I do not mean to be an alarmist nor a source of bad news. I only want to point out the obvious and restate what is a fact about what is happening in our world today.

A wave of the thoughts of fear, sorrow, and hatred is growing in the world. We have to get ready and be awakened from our sleep to confront such a wave of darkness that is coming our way from a disturbed part of the world with a perturbed vision of life. We need to be aware of the love that has brought us to this level of evolution and protect it from the destructive wave that is coming our way. This wave of hatred and resentment toward love is becoming a global threat. Soon, we will be affected by such states of mind of those who have concentrated on such behavior for hundreds of years. The world is not flat, and we no longer will be able to go west. We no longer will be able to leave those who we ran from before. Soon, we will reach a point that once again we meet, and then, my friends, we will have to deal with such huge masses of hatred and resentment. That would be a moment in our lives when we need to be ready to face what we have escaped from all these hundreds of years—what we all left behind when we left the parts of the world that did not appear right to us: the religious system of thinking that once was created by humans to bring them safety and order and that now is becoming the threat to the existence of humanity itself.

There is nothing we can do to change the past. But we can learn from the past and change and create a better future. It is time to wake up. It is the time when we need to make new decisions. It is the present time because we are the ones who are living in presence.

FALSE HOPE OF THE TRUSTING

Bush Effect: If you give them something so bad for a period of time until they are "desperate," anything "disparate" after that is not as bad, looks and feels great.

As the game of chess continues between the two superpower empires—with England on one side and the Roman Catholic Church on the other—there comes a rebel who ignores this game and walks away on her high heels from the scene of action. This new rebel is called America. And everyone wants her.

We are still that sexy, strong, powerful, sophisticated, desirable nation of people that we have been for the past 200 some years. We are still what everyone around the world wants to be like. We live where everyone else in the world wants to live. We do, eat, create, watch, behave, sing, dance, fight, and live the way everyone else wants to. And we deserve this lifestyle because we have worked very hard for it. Among all who are watching us, there are those who are envious of not having it as we do, and they do something about it, something very selfish. They want to take away what we have put together after all our hard work for their own advantage

So, the church and Churchill get up and walk after the sexy America. It is more like a chase. On the way, they push each other to the side, pull each other back, step on one another, bite each other, strangle each other, and as they see America advancing further, they get up, shake hands and make plans how to catch up to America. Although they both want America for themselves, they have a tacit agreement to remain allies until they take over America. From then, it will be the battle between the Bad and the Ugly.

England believes this very naughty child is a creation of its own, and therefore claims an ownership of her. After all, it is the money from the English-supported pirate ships that has been invested in this new country. And it is the unruly, unappreciative British colonists and their followers and descendants who now have to be punished for taking English investment away—the investment the English ships took away from all others, mainly the Roman Catholic Church of Spain, on the water of the oceans, and in the villages on the beaches of exotic lands in the sixteenth and seventeenth centuries. At the same time the American colonies detach themselves from England, England as a global superpower starts losing its territories and power due to a stretched out army and navy and a collapsing economy that feeds the army and the navy far beyond the financial capabilities of the empire. England is suffering from hunger and famine, and in the eyes of England, America is at fault.

England has to strike back to regain its global position. Plans are put together, plans that will take a long series of double-crossing actions. This is the plan of England; England's first step has been to create a global animosity toward America by telling and convincing everyone that America stole everyone's money. It already has achieved this.

The next step has been for England to teach all Muslim nations how to fight America—"the evil, the dirty, the bad woman," the rebel that has to be punished and destroyed. That's what the Muslims think of America, and England uses that. That is the mob that works for England, the Muslim mobs. Well, they have started and almost finished this step also. They trained the Ottoman Muslim sailors in the Mediterranean Sea to attack American vessels in the late eighteenth and nineteenth centuries. They gained influence in the Middle East Muslim countries to eject American influence in the region in the twentieth century. And, now, they have become the bridge for many Muslims to migrate into America in waves.

Furthermore, standing next to her, England encourages and involves America in wars that will result in the same misfortune England once suffered: a stretched out army and navy and a collapsing economy that feeds the army and the navy that is too far beyond the financial capabilities of the country. England went through such hardship while losing America in the eighteenth century, and now England is determined to bring the same adversity to America. This part of the plan is well on its way.

England has learned how socialism can help keep people under control, so it plans to implement socialism into America. This may take the most time. America has always been leery of the socialist thoughts and system. However, if in the long run it appears the benefits of having a socialist government outweigh the benefits of fighting it, then the public can be convinced to change its way of life and ide-

ology of freedom. As English politics always plays very cleverly, a sly, smart, and convincing leadership can change the gears under its dictatorship.

There will be an increased flow of Muslims into America. The rise of the Muslim population becomes so evident that elections would focus on pleasing Muslim communities. This is the infiltration of the English-run Muslim mob.

English banks get ready to come to the rescue of America when American institutions are down on their knees. On the other hand, the church also offers increased community support and social guidance, as well as family counseling for the troubled ones in the time of economic desperation. The church actually is continuing a two millennium chase that has not come to an end—a chase after a large sum of valuable, high precious metal that eventually came into the possession of America some time ago; a chase that brought Columbus to the shores of the Caribbean islands and opened up America to other immigrants.

The church and England play the (ugly) friend, (bad) friend game with America to convince her of their proof of affection to her more than the other, while still making plans hand in hand behind the scenes—at least for now. As the result of their joint plan, there will be a candidate who will sweep us off our feet—something new, something extraordinary—someone who is closer to the Muslim world in appearance yet is connected with the church.

At the end, the church and England will wrestle in the championship for the possession of America. After all, The Roman Catholic Church wants its money back, the stolen money it was taking from all the] subjugated people of Europe, and then lost that income once the noble people of Europe migrated to America. England will utilize the American Constitution to arouse people against the involvement of religion within the government. The church relies on its influence within the people's credulous minds and hearts to gain a mass of followers who will look to the pope for guidance and support. Their vehicle is placing social taboos and guilt and family planning within the society. Our responsibility in confronting this upcoming cunning master plan is to remain alert, awake, and aware. We are at a point when we must change the direction that our politics, the White House and Congress are taking us. We must act now.

In order for a society to change the direction of its standard of living, the members of that society need to find and resolve the fundamental causes of this difference. That means they need to find solutions. In order to find solutions, we first need to choose those questions that would guide our minds in a direction from which eruption of the answers would create a path of resolution for our challenge. Open up your heart to whom you really are. Open up your heart to your desires. And open up your heart to your soul. Open your mind's eye.

America must walk away on her high heels again.

COME OUT AND PLAY PLEASE

America at its core soul is constructed on show business. Everything is done to make people feel good; that is, whatever can be done that would make people feel good is a chance to make a sales transaction. If you make them feel good, you can make some money. That is human nature. And the whole system provides support socially and financially to any new show business material. This new show material should be different from previous ones, according to people's moods at a particular time.

So, there will be a need for new material that can draw attention to itself for what people need at that time. This way, people's attention is drawn to a focus that will serve as a comfort zone for them even if the focus is untrue.

This entertainment has been part of human societies from the very beginning. Unfortunately, until not too long ago, people did not care if the source of the focus of the entertainment was true or not. Many myths and hoaxes came into the picture of show business that did not have any truth in it. They were sold as the nighttime stories that would become the realities of the darkness of the night to the children. Soon after, those children would grow up believing that the scary stories of ghosts and monsters of the night that were told to them were real. This gave rise in many tribes to the tribal war songs and dances in Africa. And the wars would begin.

As human societies evolved, entertainment became a privilege for high-class society. Fortunately, about 200 years ago, people in the New World started disbelieving this type of show business. You no longer had to be a king or a queen or have a royal family connection to have access to well-presented entertainment. A constitution was written and, according to this constitution, although not always practiced, all humans are equal and have the same possibilities to entertain and be entertained and, in the same process, make some money— some money for everyone, because everyone can have the opportu-

nity to be a king or a queen. So, everyone needs to be free and enjoy the show, because, in this new show business, everyone is equal to everyone else.

So the audience will come in masses, as they did 2,000 years ago to follow the message of living within great feelings brought by a local rebel. They saw a show that was not played before and they went crazy after it. Why? Because it was a message, a story, a show that was bringing hope and happiness to their lives. So, it was sold for a great price. And, in between, many people involved in this show business made or are making money.

Is this wrong? Well, I don't think so. As humans, we have learned that the way we would want to live is a comfortable safe life. That is why an order was brought into societies. The king of the cave became the king of the country. Everything was given to him or her to provide balance in the territory. He or she could have anything as long as he or she was strong enough to protect the people. But soon, these kings became corrupt. They wanted absolute power and absolute power brought with it absolute corruption. That is what goes wrong in any show business.

This is the struggling challenge we are facing in America, to change the show business to bring more of the truth to the children who are listening to the stories. Entertainment must maintain a purpose, a direction to keep it meaningful and constructive. Entertainment also can be damaging if the content is focused on fear and hatred and injustice. We have a purpose in the core of our system, and that is the Declaration of Independence. All our efforts in all years have been to keep the light of freedom burning. And that is a responsibility we have accepted by being Americans and living in America.

So far, we have done a pretty good job. Do not get me wrong. Many mistakes have taken place. Many people got hurt unjustifiably in the process. Many lessons had to be learned about our primary human instincts and many of those behaviors and beliefs had to be changed before we started learning about our own weaknesses. Yes, in this process, many got hurt. Nevertheless, we are traveling a pathway in human evolution that can bring us all as a whole union to the destination of justice and freedom that we all seek to reach.

However, this continuing growth in the path of our evolution can only go on by the choices that we make that would keep us on this right pathway—the pathway through which we get involved in relationships with others around us through which we can make friendship and create a loving and respectful opportunity to create better lives for everyone. This opportunity can be found at work with coworkers, at a supermarket with other shoppers, with the customers and clients who come to our store or place of work, on the way home on the highways and streets, and at home when we are spending precious time with our families and loved ones. It is the value of our friendship and relationships with others that reveal the extent of the effects of the power of the universe in our lives.

Once we realize the value of friendship in our lives with the people we care about, we can recognize the level of love that we can have among us. However, we have to be careful not to repeat the mistakes of the past in our relationships throughout history. Many of us unfortunately make mistakes in our relationships. That is, we forget the value of this simple act of humanity, the value of making friends and friendship.

Remember when you were a child, or have you seen how children are together on an ice skating ring or in a park or at the beach? They make friends very easily, because they are open to the world. And they learn valuable lessons from it. They hold hands, play hide and seek, and laugh together, and give each other little kisses. How do we forget this as we grow up? What is it replaced by, and where does it go?

Perhaps we tend to close up to the continuous incoming numbers of individuals who might carry other motives in their approach when they try to make a connection with us. Or perhaps we see a limited time or different priorities with different friends and acquaintances. That is natural and understandable. We will talk more about this subject in the chapter of "Pyramid of Friendship" in the book *Pi, a Pathway to Life.* (*Pi, a Pathway to Life* was going to be published prior to the current book you are reading. But, I felt it was more important to do this book first prior to the *Pi.* That is why I do have to refer to that book from time to time.) But what we are talking about now is how we connect with others when we encounter a social circumstance.

In social circumstances, that mostly involves financial contracts and agreements for different services or work. If one is hired both by a friend and a stranger for similar work at the same time, it appears that the contract signed with the stranger would gain more attention. This is a mistake that takes place because of the level of trust we feel we need to gain with people we do not know. We tend to believe that our friends know us and have trust in us; therefore, they understand and give us credit when we are busy with other cases and have limited time to give their cases priority. In addition, a stranger is more likely to complain or even sue for lack of attention.

So, as humans in our societies, we always try our best to attend to what we can do for others who do not know us as well, to give them the motivation and opportunity to get to know us. Most times, this great attention redirects our focus from our relationship with our friends and loved ones. This lack of attention is felt greatly by those friends and loved ones. Nevertheless, we expect that our friends and loved ones understand the reason for this lack of attention and, not only are they not bothered by it, but they understand us in the situation and give us more opportunity to pay even less attention. After all, they need to help us gain the trust we are seeking from strangers.

But it doesn't work that way. What ends up happening is that our friends, our loved ones, feel ignored and start pulling away. This reaction causes a distance in the connection of the friendship, and not too long after that we wonder why they are distant from us. Most times, what ends up happening is a lot of finger pointing and blaming of each other for the lack of interest in the relationship. Needless to say, complaint and blame can only reduce the strength in the bridges of friendship.

That is why many come to this misunderstanding that partnerships or working with friends ends up with destruction of the friendship itself. However, the true cause for the destruction of the friendship is the lack of attention to this very need for friendship at crucial moments. Those crucial moments are the moments necessary for even more attention to the partnership or work. Perhaps it is accurate to say that, in reality, we can test the true depth and integrity of our friendship with our friends by becoming partners with them in a social financial circumstance.

A friend is a person whom we can trust and rely on in the moments we need help and attention. But a friend also is someone we choose to go to when we need that help and attention. A friend is one who would hold our hands when all goes wrong in our world. Clearly, a friend who asks for our professional help also must receive our utmost attention. In return, in those circumstances, a friend should understand the extent of attention he or she needs to have regarding the financial responsibilities that would accompany the services rendered to them. This giving care and attention must always be in mutual balance.

Making friends and gaining friendship is like developing a network, a web in life, and a web of life. That is the reason we all try to find new friends throughout our lives, because it is through this process of seeking and making friends that our web of life expands to new limits. It is in this web of life that all the cords connect.

We have to keep in mind that making friends does not mean overlooking the wrongdoing of others just to create a friendly atmosphere when we are interacting with them. It also does not mean we have to put up with and make compromises with people who claim they are our friends but do something intentional to harm us. Sometimes, some of us try to avoid confrontations because we are concerned so much about how others might feel or think about us that we overlook the respect we owe to ourselves. Sometimes, we might think that by not responding to someone's wrongdoing, he or she will change or go away and the problem will resolve itself. Perhaps, one of those ways might sometimes work.

However, we need to keep one thing in mind about rules of friendship. The first and foremost rule is that a friendship or interest in a friendship must be mutual. If, in any situation, we see that one lacks the interest and respect that is necessary to build a relationship, we should not be overextend any efforts to try to create a pleasing and friendly environment with that person, until he or she is ready to accept a mutual respectful relation. This does not mean that we have to reflect back a wrongful behavior. It means that we have to be aware of situations in which we offer our friendship and interest. A web of friendship can be developed and sustained only if the bonds of friend-ship are mutually desired.

Therefore, we have to test our friendship and its solidity at periodic intervals. This is done to remind ourselves of the importance of the foundation we are creating for our lives and to insure a clear vision of what our goals are in life. It also reminds us how important it is to keep the bonds we have already made. After all, our livelihood is the web of life we are creating for ourselves. Above all, we need to remind ourselves that we cannot force friendship on anybody. So, we have only two choices: either to come to an agreement toward build-ing friendships with others in ways that bring respect to all, or to choose to limit our friendships as soon as we realize the respect—of privacy, opinions, well-being, desires, dreams—is not mutual. Let us first look to ourselves at what we do every day.

HUSH, WE ARE EVOLVING

It is crucial to remind ourselves why we have chosen the occupation that we perform every day of our lives. Have we kept intact the philosophy and the purpose that brought us to this occupation to serve our world community? Do we still remember it, and do we still keep it alive in our lives? Also, we have to evaluate to see if the occupation that has been assigned to us is based on a philosophy of teamwork to create better lives for all who are a part of this team. I am not talking about a secret society. I am talking about all living beings living together in harmony and peace, seeking ways to improve the lives of all equally to reach happiness and ultimate joy—a team that is continuously at work to keep the best of harmony for everyone; a team that has the best interest of everyone in mind, to raise the standards of living for all to reach happiness.

So, it is very important to evaluate ourselves and see if we are utilizing our social, professional, and personal situation and position in an abusive way. The abuse of our position and authority in our society is the same as abusing a friendship. Abuse of a friendship is the greatest reason that the friendship would dissolve—the very friendship that is the connection that creates, strengthens, and expands our web of life, the same web of life that has brought us together as a society.

How can we remind ourselves of this very important yet hard to remember fact of life? I believe it all can be rejuvenated by celebrating life. We need to celebrate our connecting friendships. We need to learn how we can grow this extensive source of power within ourselves. And we need to learn and remember how to cherish our friends and our friendships at all different levels of our lives.

But who has time to do all of this? As our lives have grown so complex and time consuming, we find less and less time to spend with our loved ones. Making new friendships and expanding the net of friends would attract even less attention. Most of us these days would say, "I just don't have enough time to do this." And I would like to ask just this question: If you do not spend the time in your life with your loved ones and make an effort to find new friends on daily basis, then what do you spend your time doing, and why?

We have created a life for ourselves that appears to be very complex. Most times, for many of us, we have wrongfully allowed this complexity to make our lives complicated. Every day, we ask ourselves the motives for what we are doing in our lives, and most of us do not have a solid answer. It appears that, once again, we have to face the fact that if our lives are complicated, it will not give us the clear vision of the purposes we are living for. After all, if anything is not simple, it cannot reveal the truth.

Okay, let's say I have convinced you that we do need to develop friendships with others we come across in our daily lives. How do we do so? The answer is very simple, and you probably have heard it before. I am going to say it anyway. All we need to do to create friendships with others is to communicate with them in the clearest manner. We cannot make any connections with anybody if we cannot skillfully communicate with them. We can only build bonds of friendship with the ones who are not afraid of us. And the only people who are not afraid of us are the ones who have chosen to remain our friends once they have become more knowledgeable of our true intentions in life. If they remain fearful and hateful toward us once they know our intentions, then they will never become our friends anytime in the future.

Remember what knowledge is, as we talked about it in the beginning of this chapter? Knowledge is the finding of possibilities and availabilities that are constantly resurfacing, waiting to be discovered and utilized to improve our lives and our paths of evolution. This knowledge that exists among friends can only continue if the lines of communication are present. That can bring us to a higher standard of living with our friends. Therefore, we can say that communication is the most effective tool for raising the standards of living and keeping its balance intact.

Imagine a network of computers that connect and interconnect and exchange information. Let's agree that the function of equipment and the network based on those computers would rely on the amount of accurate information that is exchanged between these computers. Therefore, a communication that takes place between the heads of computers would determine the actual output and the function level of working units, equipment, and the network. The communication necessary for this performance relies on the decision-making ability of the computers, which do so based on the information given to them.

So, the accuracy of information exchanged determines how successfully the whole factory would perform and function as a unit. Now, let's think of our own societies as units. The exchange of information among the people who are performing the unity or the society determines how successful the whole factory or the organization would function as the unity. Nevertheless, the function of each building block of the unity or the society would improve as the quality and quantity of the information given to them increases. So, what we are saying is that as the information given and exchanged among people approaches accuracy and increases in quality and quantity, each person would evolve in that society. This improvement in the progress of evolution of people would cause the elevation of the society as one. Elevation and evolution of a society would return an output of function that would create high standards of living for all the building blocks of its unity.

Therefore, the quality of our communication as friends, acquaintances, teachers, families, and coworkers would determine the quality of the information that we are exchanging among us. The quality of this information determines the quality and direction of a future that a society or a people will have ahead of them.

Since most of what we learn is through the exchange of the information via our conversations in a classroom or listening to educational talk shows and tapes, or so on, we always should focus on and question the accuracy of the topic we are talking about. We also need to know that we should recognize that older and less accurate information should be replaced by newer and more accurate information on a regular basis. If we as building blocks of a society would seek to exchange and replace old inaccurate information with newer and more accurate information, then we have placed our progress in the path of our evolution to higher levels of life mentally, socially, spiritually, and financially.

This is all about the conversations we have with each other at work, in the park, on the street, and in the car. But, what makes us communicate in a certain matter with others? Why do people communicate in different manners, and why do we sometimes communicate without much success? So now, we have reached the subject of the basis of communication. What truly is communication and how can it achieve results that could improve our lives? And how should we do it without exposing ourselves to possible dangers and traps that might lie ahead in this road of openness and friendliness? Let's play a little game to find out the true sources for accurate communication.

I call this game our own hide-and-seek. Find a quiet place like a room in the library or a park, a riverside, or a beach, somewhere you would not be interrupted by distractions in the middle of what we are trying to do here now. But, first and foremost, you have to keep yourself open to wanting to play this game to find what you can learn about yourself. If you are not ready to open yourself for this search, it will not work. It all depends on you, at this point. To play this game of search successfully, first you need to open up your mind and prepare your brain to accept and absorb new information and knowledge. So, let's do this before we go to the next step.

Okay, now that you have done what we agreed on, and I hope you are being true to yourself, let's get started. All through this game, you have to realize there is no one else around you but the ones you want to be there. If you are alone, then you are the only one there to know what you will find. If you cannot be yourself when you are alone, then you have a problem facing and accepting yourself, which is something that we can work on later on in this book, because the only way you can be as strong as you want to be is by knowing your weak points and trying to fix them. My goal is to help you find that ultimate strength, so please play along.

The best way to play this game is to read and understand fully what I am asking you to do here. Then, after you have read it a couple of times, you can do it on your own. Here is how it goes. As you are sitting quietly in your secluded place, realize who or what is surrounding you. If you feel there are more sources holding you in your material presence, distinguish them and detach from them. Start forming your body by choosing one part of the body and detaching the sensations of that part of your body from your mind. As you are doing so, keep in mind that you are in the process of a hide-and-seek game. You will look for what is hiding and then you go and gather it.

Start by detaching your extremities in your mind. You have to visualize them in your mind and their connection to your body. Think of all the information that extremity brings into your body and all the memories it holds. Detach all that is within that part of your body. Start with your toes and your feet. Come up to your legs and move to the upper regions. As you are visualizing in your mind the detachment you are making from those parts and all that is contained within them, you will find a sensation rising up. As you are lying down or sitting up on a comfortable chair, you will find yourself lighter than ever.

I want you to be aware but not focus on this lightness of being growing as you detach other parts of your body. Release your fingers, your hands, and your arms, and all they contain. Get rid of the memory of pain, pleasure, and touch that is within them. And send in the power of life that is within them to the core of your body.

Next, I want you to shut your ears and all the information they are bringing to you. Your eyes are closed, so you have shut out the visual stimulations that blinded you from yourself. As you do so, I want you to bring the life power that you are keeping in the core of your body and bring it up into your brain.

By now, you are almost there. Focus now on the power that is accumulating within your brain. That is all the physical power you possess. And it is waiting for you to use it to find something that is connecting you to life itself.

I want you to feel and understand this power of life that is within your brain, and then condense it into one mass that is pushed out of your brain into the location of your mind. Your mind is an entity that resides outside your body and above your skull. Find this location and understand it. What you now are encountering is you. This is you and all that is the purpose for what your body is there for you to provide. What you find is for you and may apply only to you. Remember it and cherish it. You are now conversing with yourself—the greatest conversation that has no physical expression.

You might need some time and some practice before you fully come to realize the power you possess within your physical and spiritual body. This is the foundation for the system of questioning. I encourage you to spend a few hours a day thinking and using the system of questioning. I hope you continue on this journey of self-acknowledgment until you reach the levels of conversation with self. After all, a life without a purpose is a life wasted. More so, if you cannot have a conversation with yourself, how can you contemplate what you can communicate with others?

Have you ever had a dream when you did not know where you were or what you were doing, and, nevertheless, you did not know the end of the dream? It is like you did not have any control over what was happening in the dream. And that is why you were getting restless and scared. Scared of what? Scared of the unknown. You, just like most people, would say, of course, I've had these dreams all of the time.

We all have dreams when we are sleeping that would place us in an unknown situation with an unknown ending. However, we all wonder why, if the dreams come from our own minds, how come we do not know how they might end? If we did know how the dream was going to end, why would we be uncomfortable or scared as the dream neared its end? And what exactly is an ending of a dream? Is there a specific time or place for that? Is there a point of discomfort that we need to get to in order to finish the dream?

Dreams, as we know, stem from the observations of the mind in a day or throughout our lives. Dreams are an analysis of the information that consciously and subconsciously has been gathered by our minds. Dreams basically are a result of the work of our minds. Well, if the dream is coming from our own mind, how come we do not know what might happen in that dream?

There are two parts to our mind: conscious and subconscious. All that we are aware of is the conscious mind. All that we know but are not aware of that exists in our minds is the subconscious mind. Everyone has a conscious and subconscious mind. As we grow up in our human process of life, we exchange more of the subconscious mind for the conscious mind. As we grow, at the beginning, we have perhaps very little or no conscious mind. When we are just babies, we have a set of instincts or subconscious information that enables us to survive. It is necessary information that we need to survive. As we grow up, we are taught how to process information that is given to us through our teachings and learning at home by our parents and at school by our teachers. So, the amount in the conscious mind rises.

As our conscious mind rises, we tend to do two things. One is that we learn more about the world around us and build a conscious mind that has no limit in its learning. The other is that we become less aware of the subconscious mind that exists within us and has many capabilities and much information.

Our nightmares are a reflection of our bodies trying to make us aware of our subconscious mind. If we have many nightmares, that means we have greatly ignored our subconscious mind. The path in our evolution can continue only as we understand and are aware of our subconscious mind. It can continue and grow as we bring a subconscious mind into a conscious mind. It is that continuous self-search for what is deep down inside of us that enables us to understand our subconscious minds and ourselves.

The proportion of our conscious mind to our unknown subconscious mind is the level of evolution we have reached. The more of our subconscious minds we become aware of, the higher level of evolution we have reached.

A GOLDEN CAGE IS STILL A CAGE

There is a balance that remains between the misinformation of past parental authority and new information given by the right leadership. This balance is the battle between the internal force of traditions of a family versus the external teachings of a progressive oriented system of education—a system of the balance between the seeking of knowledge and the fear of the unknown. The more information given for a constructive and progressive direction to the new generation, the better results time will achieve in naturally eliminating infected minds of the past.

This balance has been demolished in Iran. The balance has vanished by an ancient dogmatic shift of the paradigm in the structure of the truth. The external force that should remain as the vehicle for the mutation of the minds away from the traditional culture of ignorance is the source of ignorance itself. The external source responsible for providing the new information to the new generation has been the radical fanatic minds of the past that are changing the new generation for the worse. They not only do not help provide support for new generations yearning for the change, but also help press families to teach the young about the ignorant superstitions of the past.

But the question remains: how can we ever change such a complicated and false vicious cycle of destruction of minds. Well, first and foremost, I have to remind you that if something is not simple, then it is not the truth. If any solution loses its complexity from a sense of simplicity to a state of complication, then it would not represent the truth that would set those minds free. Solutions could be as noninvasive yet ineffective as a remote presentation of education, often called "learning by osmosis," which often represents the teachers as the outsiders, or could be as extreme as a military occupation that would represent the occupants as the attackers to the heart of the existence of the society itself. As necessary as the military occupation would seem in a situation dealing with a dangerous society such as Iran, it would not resolve the infection on its own.

The new generation has to be separated from exposure to the old minds, and will need to be educated and directed to a new constructive set of values and infrastructure, one that is unknown to the old generations—a new infrastructure based on happiness and respect of privacy, one in which liberty is given to all to speak their minds, but no attention is given to the requests of the old generations. There would be no attention, because there would be no place for the old morose behaviors. All that desperately needs to be done at this stage is to provide a long school day full of excitement, happiness, games, food and snacks, and naptime for all children attending the school. This sudden change in the infrastructure of an infected society would place that society in such shock that it would create a mind-set of acceptance in those who are ready to change—those who are happy with the events they are experiencing: the children. Soon, they would learn to ignore the wrong teachings of the past and accept the ways of the future. However, this jolt would create a wave of rejection and repulsion for the ones who are afraid of the change.

We are not living this life to judge if the future is wrong or right. We need to understand that by living in an honorable way, we always will achieve a future that is fills our minds with satisfaction in our evolution. If we decide to invade any part of the world in the name of bringing a better future to the world, we have to be ready to commit ourselves to the efforts and expenses that this responsibility of teaching the children would bring upon us. If we decide that a central governing source in a society is misleading its members to an extent that its harvest would create danger of a global infection, we must be prepared to invest our time and money in providing a daily, year-round, education/recreational center for the children to attend to for a long period of time. The rest will be the work of time to heal infected minds.

We have a hard road ahead of us. The resolution of infected Middle Eastern societies is not a simple spoon-feeding of famished fools. This infection will not go away if we do not do anything. The danger not only will remain but also will gain force if the paradigm of their existence hangs about the destruction of progressive minds. And simple destruction of their central government that plays the misinforming external force in their society will not be a sufficient blow to the infrastructure that constantly gives birth to infected generations after generations. We need to understand we are facing a challenge that will change our lives altogether. And the time is approaching. Now is the time to stop this manifestation from its growth.

It is now because evolution is taking place "right now." Evolution is taking place at all moments of life. Every single moment that is moving along is the path in the building of the foundation for what is to come next. There is no destiny. There is only the formation of what we have put down and have built upon. Whatever happened in the past is the basis for the evolution of what exists now. Different events can happen in different parts of the world. And those differences are the causes of the difference in the path of evolution for different living beings in different parts of the world. We can see this difference in the physical aspects of the species that evolved in isolated parts of the world, such as Australia or New Zealand or Madagascar. Although those species grew at the same rate as others around the world, they took a different path of evolution. That path of evolution was separate from the path of evolution the species of the connected lands went through as one.

The evolution of minds also takes similar turns when a group of minds is isolated from the rest of the world. We can see this difference in the acts of isolated tribes living deep inside the Amazon or in Africa or China. We can see that their evolution has taken a different turn for their minds. It would be an insensitive and ignorant conclusion for us to call their differences "primitiveness." And, unfortunately, many times we do make the mistake to think of others, as "the lesser humans who did not evolve enough to be just like us The fact remains that they evolved based on whatever external influences they had around them in their lives. And they evolved exactly according to those external stimulants—no less than any other humans in other parts of the world.

The question remains: what would happen if we were to bring a newborn baby from the Amazon and bring him to San Diego and let him grow up in this new world just like all the other boys and girls who live and grow in this city? Think of an answer right now. Perhaps you are going to say he is just going to grow up like all the other kids learning how to play soccer and surf, and drive his date to the movies and study hard for his SAT. All right, agreed, but let's go back to our discussion about the difference in the paths of evolution of minds for a minute before reaching a conclusion.

The humans residing in the deep Amazon have not interacted or seen any other humans from other parts of the connected world for perhaps 20,000 years. That means their evolution has been unaffected by whatever happened in the rest of the world. During this past 20,000 years, humans in the connected world have made various dis-

coveries and have developed many ways to raise the standards of living by making a variety of tools and prescribing new technology. We
even have found ways to go into space. Some theories speculate man
may have been making fire up to 1.6 million years ago; As a matter of
fact, the migration of this specie relied upon having fire with them.
Otherwise, traveling to new territories at night with all other large
hunters would not be a successful one. Also, our social evolution and
skills have had deep roots more than just a 20–100 thousand year of
history. But, the early man could not make fire, rather could keep fire.
A fire in a camp ground would have to continuously be kept lit, and
the new fire would be made by transporting a flame from this source.
It was only until recently when humans learned how to start a fire. As
humans who were not even capable of starting a fire on a snap 20,000
years ago, we have developed to become humans who break the sub-
atomic layers to obtain energy. So, obviously, we have changed during the past 20,000 years. However, you and I and every other
intelligent human knows that if we bring that newborn child from the
Amazon and teach him or her all that we know and can offer, we
would end up having an intelligent young person who could change
the standards of living for all others by the discoveries he or she could
arrive at as a scientist or an artist.

Then, all this time having different effects on different humans
has not meant anything but opportunities for us to learn about ourselves and what is around us in different aspects. That means that the
evolution of humans' minds is currently separated and unaffected by
the evolution of humans' bodies. Nevertheless, we need to realize
that as a side effect of evolution of mind, the body also will change
in shape and manner. So, the changes that have taken place in
humans in different parts of the world have nothing to do with their
physical bodies. Rather, it has to do with the external influences that
have caused them to reach different mental levels already existing
within them. Through this achievement of self-acknowledgement,
competition in utilization of technology available to them has pushed
them to find and accept the abilities that are within them in shorter
time intervals.

Humans are not so different in their evolution of the body or brain
from each other in different parts of the world. They are only different
in the "utilization of the physical abilities" encoded within them. This
difference stems from the difference in the environmental stimulants
around them. We do not have a prescience of what different humans
would become based on the behavior of previous generations or the

physical characteristics; rather, we can be certain that external influences can create different paths of evolution in the human mind. That difference in the minds of humanity is what will make a different life for different people simultaneously around the world in the present and a different set of precursors for a proximate or distant future for all others who are affected by that present.

The problems that have made the societies in Middle Eastern areas weak and unstable are the external factors they have allowed their lives to become important. It also is the lack of some of the most important human rights that have not been built into their developmental foundation—a foundation that is necessary to carry on the growth process in an evolutionary path that would be sustainable and healthy for all living beings residing on this planet. The challenge they are experiencing is a self-inflicted disability they have brought into their own "web of life." The fact remains that no matter what direction we choose to go in our "web of life" on earth, we all will go on as one group of living beings evolving together in some manner and for some time. But if we cannot establish a harmony among us as humans, nature will do that for us in a way that will be different than what we have chosen now and perhaps in a jolt that would seize our patterns of life as we know it forever.

The right thing always will happen, prescribed by the powers of nature for endurance of nature. But nature's prescription might not always be so favorable to us humans if we are not in accordance with it. It is our responsibility to learn from nature and provide the harmony necessary to sustain within its "web of life." Looking beyond our own existence would mean having a desire to provide a favorable environment for our children and their children as well. For that, we also need to think very much about finding the ways that would assure the existence of the harmonious environment at the present and future in a consistent manner paralleling the acceptance of change in periods of time.

This harmony can be best reached when all components of this "web of life" make shared collateral efforts in finding tolerance and courage necessary to overcome the ignorance that has separated us all. In addition, the Middle Eastern societies have to take responsibility to take the constructive action to rid themselves of the superstitious traditions that are keeping them away from a state of mind that provides grounds of acceptance of others and other behaviors unknown or different to them. For a start, this would simply mean that they would have to accept the word and meaning of privacy and start practicing it, and stop giving value to interfering with each other's lives from their cultures and minds.

Such acceptance and extraction would mean breaking away from some of the most necessary factors within the society that has held old traditions together. We have to be aware that without those fundamental social rules, the fanaticism that has retarded the advancement of the minds of the Middle Eastern people would no longer be a value to measure and duel on. But taking this first step is the most difficult part of moving this heavy train of events that would take place consequently. The international support and thrust is very crucial in initiating this move and helping it to continue moving to its destination of reaching collateral efforts.

Such societies need to understand the value of privacy in respecting others. They need to understand that all people regardless of their religion, race, language, or gender possess the same rights as all living beings do to make choices in their lives. No person or entity has the authority to take this right away from anyone else. Nonetheless, those who invade the privacy of others by endangering their freedom to make choices in their own lives should be confronted and disabled. The highest of all crimes is the invasion of privacy and being a burden on others' lives. This is the most destructive wrongdoing in human society and should be fought against. Invasion of privacy is an offense that becomes most detrimental to a civilization once it reaches the highest levels of leadership authorities of that society.

We have seen this corruption within many of the authorities around the world, far and near, and the seriousness of the threat they are imposing on our qualities of lives. It starts with taking away from us and getting us used to not having the basic human rights since a young age in small measures. How can we forget that when we are born, we are free souls who have nothing but the right to live and make choices for our own lives? And how can we ignore the fact that it is others who take this freedom away from the babies as they grow into the matrix of the social boundaries made by the rules of complicated religions and traditions? Religions and traditions that expose their own untruthfulness by the complications they present while separating people by the differences in the value systems they claim. Religions and traditions that put blame, guilt, and shame on the soul of the human beings from the moment they are born. We all know those religions. Those religions are the religions any of us practice in the name of serving a god, a god that has been given so much power by the very division those religions have brought to humanity in different locations.

There is no guilt; there is no shame in experiencing life in a manner that would not cause a burden on the lives of others. Everyone needs to experience life according to one's own curiosities and evolutionary paths. But some of us find another self-inflicted guilt. That guilt is the sense of responsibility to stop others from experiencing life in ways that we find fearful for ourselves. And, sometimes, some of us feel that it would make us look better if we show interest in the welfare of others even if it means invading their privacy. And many of us do this with the excuse of love, and with the concern that our retraction from invasion of privacy would only present our lack of love and concern. But I have to ask this now. Why would we worry about what others might think of us if we truly understand the meaning of privacy?

If we are worried about the observation of others of what we do and how we do it, then we have not understood the meaning of privacy. My privacy is the space I possess around me that inhibits others' observation and judgment of the behavior I choose to live by as long as this behavior does not become a burden on others and their privacy and life. If I understand this valuable integrity within my own life, then why would I care what others think of the lifestyle I choose to have? If anything, I should understand that those who are making efforts to invade my privacy should be ashamed of themselves.

I live my life and only my life. This is true for all of us. We live our lives to learn and grow from it. If we are not growing from this living we experience every day, then what is the point of living it at all? We live it to experience, and we learn by experimenting new ideas. In that experiment, we might and will make mistakes. And as Thomas Edison once said, "After this mistake, I am now one step closer to the truth."

We need to make mistakes. And we need not to be afraid of making mistakes. And we need to recognize our mistakes once we make them by learning from their results. And we need to assure not repeating those mistakes over again. It is not the mistakes that would form the direction of our lives. Rather, it is the solutions and framework we find from those mistakes that gives our lives a direction, a meaning, a purpose.

In my life, I always try very hard to remember one point ahead of me that keeps me motivated to go on with my lessons in life. I make great efforts to remember that I am the steps I take in life. Every step I take gives me a new direction and experience in life. And I know that if I become fearful of taking the next step for the reason that it might be a mistake, then I would never take any steps to go anywhere. I would just sit in my room writing about my own loneliness. If we become afraid of taking steps in life for the risk it might hold in making mistakes, our lives would lose their meaning and purpose, and our true integrity and personality would be buried under the masks that we wear to make ourselves look good. Our lives, our existence, are only the continuation of the steps we are taking in life.

NOT TIME TO BE POLITICALLY CORRECT

A successful society is one that has built a system of leadership that encourages its members to seek the answer to the very fundamental question: "Why should we become self-aware?" Such systems of leadership would result in the progress of evolution of their societies. In addition, it is the responsibility of a society to select a system of leadership that would provide guidance to continue on the pathway of evolution for the next generations to come.

On the other hand, in societies suffering from inflation, lack of regulations, disharmony and chaos, it is the leaders of such societies that are incapable of finding reason enough to influence themselves and others around them to search for truth. It is the lack of initiative by the leaders and the society for not asking and finding convincing and constructive answer to such questions as: "Why should I do what I do in a way that would improve the life of others around me just as well as my own life?" "Why should I encourage others to improve their lives?" "Why should I be concerned about others I do not know or do not affiliate with?"

To ask ourselves those questions and share our conversations with others and discuss our point of views would create a balance among the members of a society such as the Global Society. When this discussion is done in a constructive environment, it will promote growth and evolution of those societies. This environment is one in which people have freedom of speech. In societies where freedom of speech does not remain or exist, the likelihood of finding constructive answers would be reduced or demolished. Freedom of speech is the most fundamental and constructive part in the self-acknowledgment and evolution of our societies. To disrespect freedom of speech is to disrupt our own progress in the path of growth and evolution.

Having the freedom of speech is the nobility that is contained within the core of the ideology of America. America is an idea, a movement, a gathering of all who respect and demand the laws of privacy, expression of self, and freedom of experimentation. Such nobility does not exist in other parts of the world, especially not in Islam-infected communities. Its survival may very well be in danger in America as well. This nobility requires our utmost attention and cherishing to continue to thrive here in America. Or it may perish, as some members of our society are finding exploitation of others a means to entertain others even as they earn money from it.

We very easily can be those people who have formed habits to disrespect and disregard freedom of speech. The questions one must ask in such situations are: "Why should I be able to listen to others without any prejudgment?" and "Why should I disrespect and disregard freedom of speech?" A true answer to those questions can reveal the facts that would make clear the results of having or lacking freedom of speech. On one hand, we can create an environment in which the result would be happiness and comfort for all its members; on the other hand, we have a suppressive environment in which everyone is eager to step on others by dictating what only serves self-interest.

It is our choice of which answer we will have to the questions we ask ourselves. And, regardless of what we think of this freedom, we still have the right to advocate our opinion about it, good or bad, as long as our opinion does not create actions that would become a burden on others. It is this right to "freedom of speech" for each of us individually that gives us the opportunity to share our views with others, no matter what we think of freedom of speech. Freedom of speech is a universal state of being that is wrongly suppressed from time to time in our human societies in the name of manmade laws or religions.

If we have a habit of thinking a specific way, a tradition or religion, we need to ask ourselves what standard of living that tradition of living has brought us and where it is taking us. If, at any point in life, we find ourselves in situations or standards of living we are not happy with, we need to ask ourselves a simple question: "Why should I try to find new ways by which I could change my life, and what are the consequences if I do not make this effort?"

This change requires an import of ideas along with the people who carry them. The nobility of this country relies on the nobility of the immigrants who have left their home countries behind and have sought a place of gathering where all the nobles are free to experiment, learn, teach, and design for future generations. This nobility may be found within extraordinary people who helped shaping America: generals such as Washington, philosophers such as Jeffer-

son, politicians such as Jackson, attorneys such as Adams, scientists such as Einstein.

This nobility is found among the people who help carry the light of America on this journey forward—the soldiers, the civil workers, the National Guard, the Coast Guard, the immigration officers, the nurses, the doctors, the farmers, the cowboys and cowgirls, the research scientists, the postal men and women, the teachers, the animal activists, the students, the lawyers, the true journalists, the musicians, the athletes, the artists, the engineers, and the authors, among so many other important teeth on the wheels that drive America forward.

It is the nobility of the generations who have moved here, and upon which we have become noble, which has made this country what it is now. And it is important that we only allow such nobility to be our guide in selecting the immigrants who live among us. Financial prosperity of one does not have a direct correlation with this nobility and, most certainly, it must not have an influence on our decision to measure one's nobility. This decision is about self-respect and respect for the rights of others in the society, and how one is free to express the nobleness he or she may possess.

We must look within our society and evaluate the new generation of immigrants and the nobility they may or may not carry, and foresee the future of our nation as the people who have gathered to design and construct such future.

Remaining attached to one particular way of living and thinking, and rejecting any new ways by prejudgment, is an addiction one could have equally toward a substance or issue. The addiction would blind an addicted person to any other reality. An addicted person would not accept any other reality that might place the matter of addiction itself under questioning. The addiction of minds to a solitary demanding way of thinking is one of the most dangerous addictions, one that has retarded the growth and retracted the evolution of minds of humanity.

But what is addiction itself? Addiction is the failure to distinguish between a need and a desire. We have certain needs that are inescapable. We all need air to breathe. We need food to eat. We need water to drink. Our desires are to have romantic relationships, joy, happiness, sex, friendship, acceptance by others, progress, and fame. If a desire turns into a need, or it appears to be a need in our lives, then we have formed an addiction within ourselves. We are required at this point to understand the distinction between addiction and habit formation; habit formation is mainly a state of mind, whereas addiction is mostly a physical state of dependency. Habit formation is the precursor and a prelude to the addiction formation. An addiction is a physical dependency to narcotics, to a person, to work, to a tradition, to a culture, or to a religion. If you find yourself having a need for anything that is a desire, then you have to realize you have an addiction, and you have to break this addiction. And the choice is yours.

As an evolving species, we are required to make the right decisions, asking ourselves the tough questions along the way, and, while searching for the answers, surround ourselves with a healthy environment to achieve and maintain the most fundamental essence of evolution: freedom of self-expression. That place of evolution for many nobles has been the grounds and ideology of America. So, the quality of the population growth will have a direct effect on such an environment. I see a great population of Muslims who are migrating to this land, the land of America. I cannot help but ask why such a population seeks to migrate to the land of such ideology that conflicts with its core beliefs, and upon what nobility are we accepting this huge flow of this certain population in the world? Furthermore, what nobility does this community contain to add to our ideology? Are we blindly accepting anything in fear of being politically incorrect, for the dread of being criticized for our judgment? Are we behaving in a way to response to our addiction of being accepted even though it may be for the wrong reasons? Or are we just becoming too apathetic to what is being done to our ideology?

There is one sure way that is the beginning to restore our freedom, and to break away from the social matrix we have become bounded to. That is to do truly what is in our hearts, to fulfill all the desires in our minds, to make real all the thoughts and fancies we have in our guts so long as we do not become a burden to anyone else. Do what you really want to do deep inside as long as it does not cause any harm to anyone else. Be the clown that you want to be, be the sex maniac that your body always screams to be, be the open and free mind that your vision always is looking for, and be true to yourself. Listen to your body and mind and break away from the cocoon you have made for yourself in this crowded tunnel of existence. Do what is in your heart and do it with the awareness that when you truly do what is in your heart, you cannot find any room for the actions that would be a burden to anyone or anything else—because having happiness is only truly satisfying when it includes happiness for all. This would be the only way one truly can be happy, by learning and understanding life, and without getting too attached to it, getting ready to move on to higher levels of existence. It is an existence we find within this explosion of the universe, an explosion that is our medium of life traveling at warp speed within space on the pattern of PI; a pattern that is the Pathway to Life.

Spiral of Life

It is not so far from reality to say that we can see the future. As I will discuss in my next book, *Pi, A Pathway to Life*, our actions as individuals create our present and our future, the future when our children and the next generations will have to live the life we have left for them in their world. Our actions and decisions bring together all different components of our societies into a matrix that will provide or take away the personal rights and individual liberties for us and the next generations. So, by evaluating our actions as a whole today, we can see what we should expect to leave for our children tomorrow.

Our founding fathers created a complex experimental system upon which a nation of humans was put together for a mission. This nation was brought together under one united vision. The vision was to make available the freedom of expression and the liberty to quest for happiness equally for every member of the society. This is what we know as democracy today. As a result, the members of this nation have had the greatest opportunity among all other human societies to express their visions and ideas and to be the vanguard of human evolution. This was the future the founding fathers envisioned for us.

This characteristic of our society has brought a flourishing environment to its members. The difference in this new world order—that is, to seek happiness and liberty under equality—brought democracy into the world. However, it seems the nature of such a noble idea has changed through time. We are actually at a point where we have to backtrack and understand the actions and the steps our founding fathers and others after them took that brought us to this point. We also have to analyze where we went wrong, learn from the mistakes, change direction, and apply the corrections into a new future, and for the future generations. One of the main issues is the power and control we have left to the employees we call the authority of the central government.

We have to be aware that if we give the central government authority beyond what the founding fathers saw fit, we will risk the existence of any freedom by halting further development and evolution of our experiment. That is the same kind of authority that has brought the humans under a debilitating subjugation in most parts of the world throughout history. And that is not what democracy is about.

Let us first review the meaning of democracy. Democracy is a statement derived from the Greek term demokratia which means "rule of the people." Although there is no universal definition for the word democracy, such noble right contains two major components: freedom and equality. Freedom is a personal right of the members of a society protected by a constitution, and equality is the responsibility of all the members of such society toward the laws of freedom with no one having any special legal privileges. We also know that if a particular division of such a system gains and accumulates power, such weight can become devastating to the structure of democracy itself.

Furthermore, we have to be aware of the role of the government in the protection of the constitution. There is a great potential and possibility that the ones involved with the government for a longer period of time would find keeping such power of authority appealing and appetizing. This is a basic characteristic of human behavior. That characteristic is a behavior that brings tyranny upon others. Tyranny, however, needs a massive support to maintain its position and weight. Sustainability of the system of tyranny is achieved when the supportive members of its own society have a majority of one or another. Tyranny cannot maintain power unless it becomes a "tyranny of the majority." And that will of the majority, we need to understand, is not democracy.

"Tyranny of the majority" is when a central government creates an ostensible interest of the majority of the society above and superior to individual rights. A corrupt central government can only continue as long as its existence can bring financial benefit to the majority of its population regardless of what rights they may take away from some or all members. One of the major signs of a central government taking such direction is for its congress or senate, or any organization taking such position, to vote on subjects that include all citizens but exempts the organization or the congress or senate from such effect.

A complete "tyranny of the majority" would be a hard task to achieve while the basic tools of democracy still remain within a society. Those tools are freedom of political expression, freedom of speech, and freedom of the press or as we know it now, media. Just like any chain, this foundation of democracy is also as strong as its weakest link. Perhaps you know what the weakest link in that compilation would be. If you said media, congratulations, you are right.

The easiest axis of the democracy to be exploited and bought by a potentially corrupting central government is the media. In a society that is spiraling downward into tyranny, the media becomes a tool of the authoritarian central government. In such society, the media is the machine, the messenger, and the driver of the government over the population. It becomes not an investigative force, but, rather, the directing force of the government and their authorities over the masses.

As soon as such government senses a need for the masses of the public to focus on a new direction, they utilize the media to deliver the message to the masses. Although this delivery may have been a pure and justified force initially, it has now lost its true value and meaning in our corporation-run world. It has now only become an agent of the central government and the corporations that feed their ever-growing hunger for authority. The media has now become the circus that plays many shows to keep the masses mesmerized, distracted, and then aligned with the direction desired by the government. This corruption entered the world of media first when England convinced America in 1917 to establish the propaganda system known as "Four-Minute Men." The Four Minute Men were a group of volunteer public speakers who were given authority by President Woodrow Wilson to give speeches on topics given to them by a governmental agency. This agency was called the Committee on Public Information, and the topics would be a propaganda speech given at the movie theaters across the country to encourage the American public to side with England. I urge you to read about this initial blow to the integrity of the world of media. This was one of the major movements when English propaganda redirected the politics of the American people toward an acceptance of the English system within our own. Many organizations now working for the government such as IRS and Federal Reserve Bank are English organizations that were integrated into our American system at the beginnings of 20th century.

We can see that the media in America is now taking such direction upon them. First, they get us to be focused on a terror attack when the government wants us to forget about internal affairs of the corrupting financial entities and the hardship this corruption is going to bring upon society. Then, they want us to forget about the terrorists and instead get us involved with a war. That works for a while, until they see the public is getting bored. Then they throw in sex scandals and death of celebrities. As that gets old real fast, they focus on a natural disaster and make a big deal covering that disaster to distract everyone from what is going on inside the corrupting system of government. They then make us feel guilty for a while for having a better standard of living than others in the world. Since this feeling of guilt does not last among the hard-working, tax-paying public, the media digresses from the natural disaster itself and then focuses on the involvement of Americans with the subjects related to the natural disasters or war broken areas.

But this does not end right here; once they have your attention all to themselves, all of a sudden, the protection of lives of the Americans who shortly before were criticized for their involvement in those situations becomes the center of attention. It seems like that a few have to be sacrificed in the arena from time to time to keep the masses entertained. And this amusement tactic goes on and on as the public is too busy watching to notice what rights of democracy the government is taking away. The economical breakdown of the society comes at last to terrify all the good, hard-working members of the society, who had gradually begin to question the corruption of the authorities, but suddenly now have to worry about what may happen to them after they retire.

The masses become so absorbed into this show that they forget to look up and see what the government is doing. As long as the masses are entertained, they are not aware of the backstabbing, corporation-supported government that is bringing them under its subjugation. And the government finds new and more effective ways to enslave the masses deeper into the land of oblivion. The land of opportunity for everyone is now the land of opportunities for a selected group that runs the government, the beneficiaries of the corporations.

As large industrial corporations grow stronger and as the small business spirit disappears, the extent of democracy diminishes in many forms. That corruption is the halt to the system of democracy, the system that brought us capitalism. That corruption in actuality would be the end of capitalism. It seems now that the media suggests and implies that capitalism is the reason we have had the financial challenges our society is going to be facing for years to come. There are many reasons to blame the very system that has brought us forward through many domestic or foreign wars, depressions, and revolutions. Capitalism was not just something that the founding fathers brought to this land at first, no, that was democracy. We have to understand that democracy is not a by-product of capitalism; rather it is capitalism that is a by-product of democracy. Yet, we have to be aware that unlike capitalism, corporation formation is not an original byproduct of democracy, rather it is a mutation that is making the system itself ill.

The question now is how we could protect our rights and the American ideology we are putting to experimentation from any corrupting power. That is why I feel I have to quickly and briefly explain the political globe and its structure as our media and government have not explained it to the public for their own convenience. Let us first review and understand the role of different social structures and ideologies. The very first one to understand is the social structure of libertarian life.

Libertarianism is the fundamental preservation of personal rights and privacy. This practice of ideas assures self-preservation via maintenance of self-liberty and rights through the keeping of private property. The life philosophy of one living as a libertarian is to do as you wish as long as what you do does not infringe upon others and their rights. Libertarianism is the most ideal and the highest level of a human society that cannot have a set rule to abide by. For the same reason, libertarian social structure is the most challenging to achieve and maintain. This noble structure is practiced and approached by two different divisions around the world. Each part of the world has formed a social structure according to its own cultural background to reach this very righteous goal.

The most drastic approaches globally have been observed during the eighteenth, nineteenth, and twentieth centuries through the Russian and American ideologies. Each of these cultures have invested much time and money as well as human power to establish a ground solid enough to rise into the pyramid of libertarian social structure. The two cultures have competed and designed many games to succeed over the other to achieve such a utopia. Libertarian social thinking can be subdivided into anarchist and minarchist. In an anarchist system, the production of any work is owned by the workers, whereas, in minarchist system, the government is limited and small and kept to protect individual rights from theft, aggression, and fraud. In minarchy, the owner of a property is the sole owner of the private property and what comes out of it.AAA

This conception can also be further explained in a polarized version of social structures. In this picture, the strong pole of libertarian social psyche has an opposing magnetic political force. You know that the two different poles have very opposing magnetic characteristics. Now, if one of these poles is the ideology of libertarianism, the other pole would consist of something that is completely the opposite of the first one. This pole is the ideology of utilitarianism. One who practices the understanding of utilitarian beliefs wishes for the preservation of greatest good for the greatest number of people. The moral worth of an action of a person is determined by its contribution to the overall outcome for the majority. The life stance of it has its ultimate importance of happiness and pleasure for the majority, even though if it is at the cost of infringement upon the minority, or even if the majority is wrong.

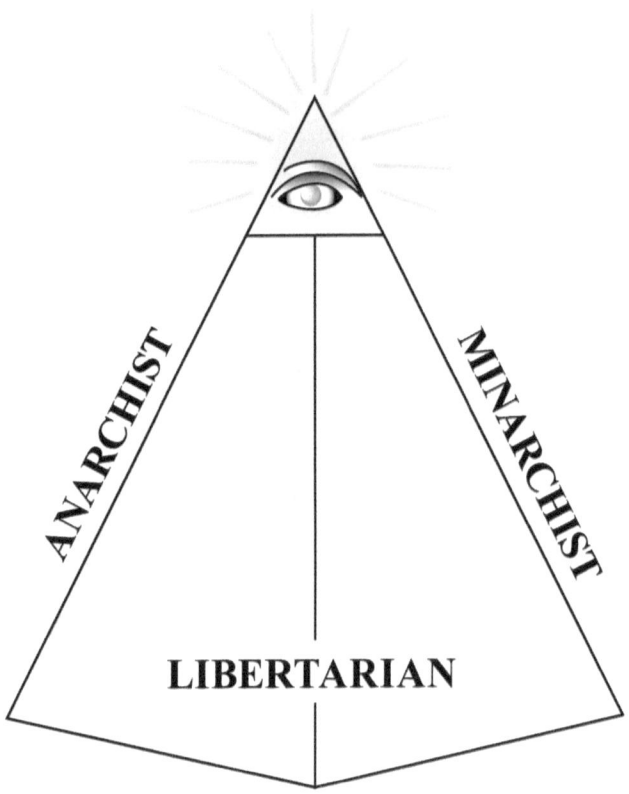

It is the attraction between the two poles that has kept all our social structures together on a global level. In order for any society to sustain the system they are surviving upon, they have to include to a certain extent all different characters of social economy and beliefs into their system. After all, the difference between a capitalist and a social society is the direction they take with the understanding of the libertarian pole. If one society leans toward anarchy, it will lean toward a communist or, at best, a socialist society. Whereas, when a libertarian ideology heads toward personal rights, individual ownership, and privacy, a society practicing such values would lean more toward a republican or democratic capitalistic society.

It is the direction of the system of libertarian thinking of a society that determines the direction of its government; to be on either side of the field of polarity balancing between the two poles of anarchy or minarchy.

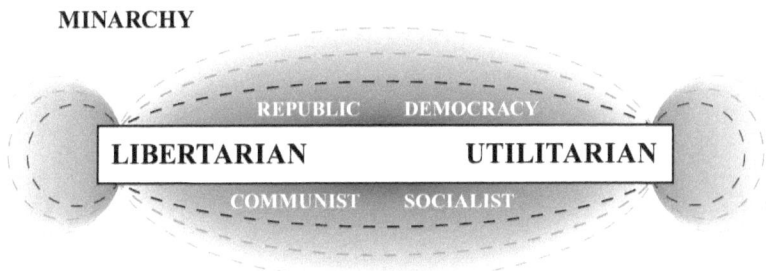

Now, let us see this diagram on a circular display of opposing characters. In this configuration, each pie of the circle opposes an opposite and polar side. For instance, "Republican" is opposed by "Socialism," and "Democratic" is opposed by "Communism" as "Libertarian" is opposed by "Utilitarian." Also, please notice that the boundaries of each pie overlap the boundaries of an adjacent pie structure. For instance, "Republican" extends into the neighboring two pies of "Democratic," and "Communism" extends into the two neighboring pies of "Socialism." Where the "Libertarian" is the umbrella to the "Republican" and "Communism" structures separating the two by a wall, the "Utilitarian" is the umbrella to the "Democratic" and "Socialist" structures connecting them as a bridge.

This proximity and correlation also explains the influences or the rejections opposing or adjacent sides can have on one another. For instance, "Republican" has a great tolerance for "Democratic" but has rejection against "Socialism." "Democratic" has tolerance for both "Republican" and "Socialism" and can act as a bridge to the two societies. Nevertheless, "Democratic" has rejection against "Communism" but can be bridged to it via "Socialism." The two pies of "Republican" and "Communism" are the two different sides of the "Libertarian" pyramid, so that, although they may coexist, they will never see eye to eye!

Now, let us utilize the structure of a seashell to explain and help comprehend the space each social structure leaves to its individual members as personal rights. As you look into a seashell, you notice a larger opening that swirls into a circular inner part that shrinks in size as it approaches the middle of this circular tunnel. The tunnel simply shrinks in size as the tunnel narrows toward the center.

The opening of the seashell is where one can experience the most amount of space to move around within the "shell." The center is

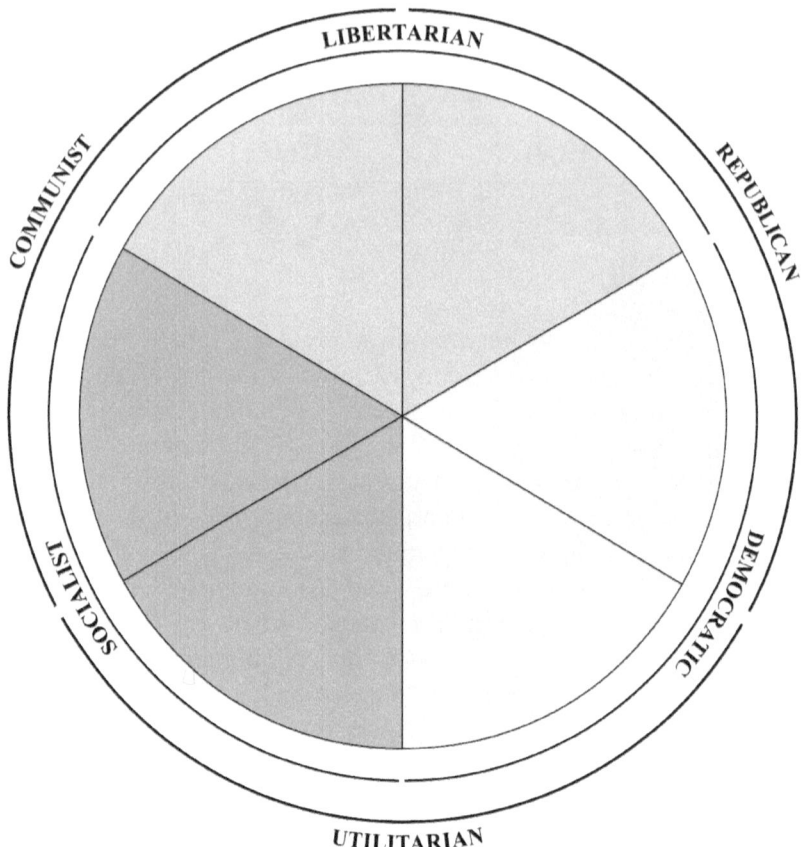

where one experiences compression and tightness where one cannot move around as easily. If we apply this structure to the circular struc-ture that I was just explaining to you a little earlier, we can see that the opening of this "sea shell" remains at the apex of the utilitarian ideology, whereas the center is at a location in the center of the circle that is indicated by letter "T" for "totalitarian." A totalitarian or authoritarian society is one where within such structure one has the least quantity of self-expression and liberty to make decisions for oneself. In the following diagram, the white area represents the quan-tity and quality of self-expression and liberty, whereas the darker areas express the control of the government over the people. This area represents individuals having to follow what they are told by their governing authority.

In case of a totalitarian government, the members of authoritarian society do not have any rights to balance themselves.

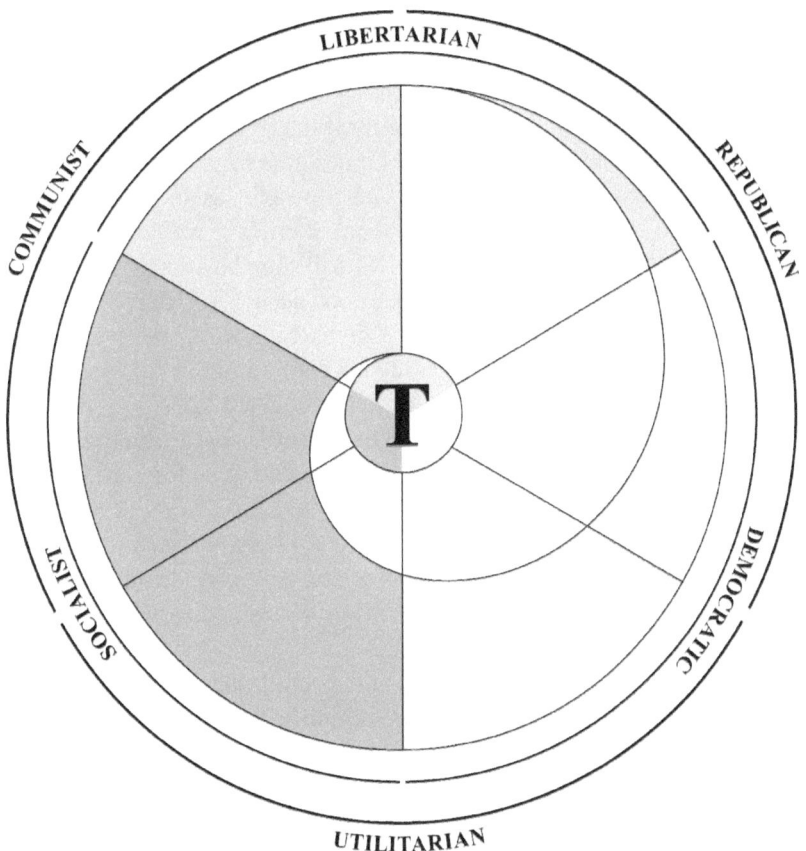

White area = personal liberty

Colored area – control of the governing authority

The motion of social acceptance of decay tends to move clockwise in our human societies. This clockwise motion is driven forward as it has been seen throughout human history. A force that has moved all societies so far in such direction is the greed of humanity. Greed is what has caused many wars, created many social and religious organizations, and formed many ways of control and subjugation of defeated societies. Before the new age of democracy, this greed was expressed via slavery of the defeated nations and torture or at least severe punishment of the rebellious ones. Such motion takes societies from any point of reference on this circle of social ideologies toward the left side of the circle. Think of the "Republican" as the right wing, where as anything on the circle moving clock-wise would be the left wing, and the greed would be the derailing force that stops a "Republican" society from achieving the ultimate "Libertarian" society.

We have lost our way from democracy and capitalism. We now live in a society that is slowly immersing itself into the deep dark waters of socialism. As a matter of fact, it is not inaccurate to say that we are now approaching the grounds of communism where, as citizens, we are frightened of losing our leftover personal liberties if we do not behave as we are told to by the government. We will soon be approaching total-itarianism if we don't stop this process of decay. Such given-up per-sonal liberties and rights may not be given back as easily ever again. The question is, are we going to do something about this slow and seemingly tolerable process of decay before it is too late?

Well, there is a carrot in front of us that we have to ignore as we realize it does not really exist. This carrot is taking us forward into, as we said before the "Land of Oblivion," where, as a mass population, we will be enslaved into a system where we have to work in the part of the social system we are designated for. The old idea of the ones behind this corruption is that we will all be trained to work for one system in one particular position.

In a system of anarchy, the lack of a central understanding of per-sonal rights of privacy and liberty is diminished and reduced although the main force is not a central government, rather a widespread system of committees. It is this lack of respect of individual privacy and liberty that can ingest the system of anarchy into a system of communism. A system that lacks offering the opportunities for individual growth and self-expression concludes into a subjugating totalitarian system.

In post-democratic societies, this subjugation takes a new form. This motion is carried via a new and upcoming Empire called "Large Industrial Corporations." Such corporations have slowly diminished the security of the farmers and their agricultural independence, and have relocated them into larger cities. This relocation creates a larger mass of people who become dependent on a larger government that dictates what everyone's position in society should be.

Now, you may ask what force moves a society from a democratic, republican, or even libertarian structure toward socialism, commu-nism, and eventually, totalitarianism. That force is greed.

Corporations are the vehicles that feed the greed of the power-seeking men and women of so-called governing authorities, which take us on a journey, at best, in a clockwise direction from the prox-imity of libertarian ideology toward totalitarianism. And corporations have been at work for more than a century in America.

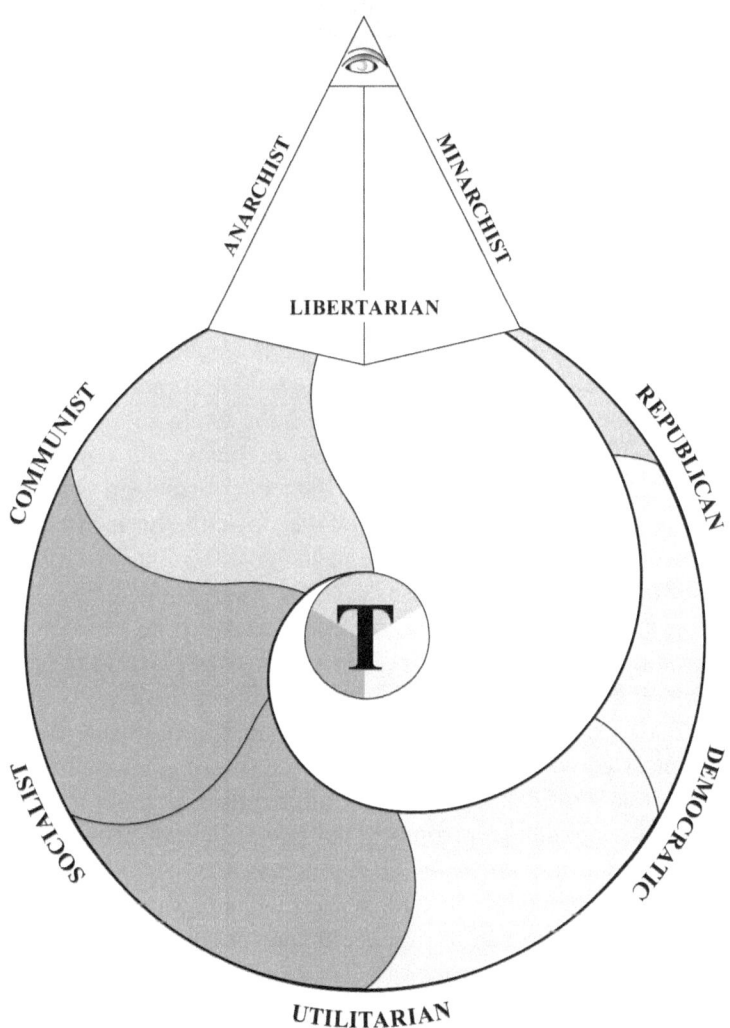

Large corporations that run food, agricultural, energy, pharmaceutical, banking and real estate industries are major components of the supply and demand of the wheel of corruption. This wheel of corruption has been turning us away from the American vision and ideology the founding fathers planned and designed for future generations. These industrial companies are now major components of the governing authorities, a government (not of the people) that is gaining increasing strength and influence every year in America.

What has become an imperative problem is that the same people who benefit from the corruption of the corporations are holding the key positions in the government, which hold responsibility for the investigation of such corruption. As a matter of fact, large industrial corporations have a great influence on the outcome of the election of many members of congress and other elected officials. Some of these corporations are Tyson, Wal-Mart, Monsanto, Exxon, BP, Merck, Fannie Mae, Meryl Lynch, Goldman Sachs...they have attached themselves so deeply into the system they can threaten that they will let the system fail if we go after their corruption.

So, as the profit-minded food industry causes diseases such as diabetes, another profit-minded industry—pharmaceuticals—jumps in to provide medication to control the disease. The corporations are not focused on the cause of the illness, but on the product they can sell to the public. These companies orchestrate problems and then provide relief from the symptoms to support their businesses and profit margins. This causes great harm to society, and such harm is not investigated or stopped because the people in charge of leading investigations benefit from the sales of products the corporations manufacture.

These are the con artists, the "snake oil sales people," who are taking advantage of the trust the people of America place in their government, and then selling them out by promising them values which do not really exist for their investments. Their approach and presentation is most convincing for the people of America. By definition, a con man is a confidence man who confidently lies about his or her true intentions to sell something to the public in confidence with the knowledge that they are lying. A con person lies with confidence in such delivery that people believe in the false integrity of the con artist. Once they make people believe in that integrity, then they can steal from them in many ways.

Although this terminology started over a hundred years ago, describing the unethical men who would rob hopeful people out of their hard-earned money, today, such men and women use their art of lying in confidence to gain political and social advantages. They deliver messages of hope based on false information to a public whose apathy and disinterest in true politics has made them dependent on government to secure and satisfy their addictions.

The government that was put in place to protect us from harm has turned to the agency that provides a cover-up for the corrupt corporations so they can continue enslaving their consumers, we, the people. In return, the ones in government help the corrupt corporations get the finances and support that helps them stay in their positions. Our greed is being used against us to bring us into a comfort zone for addiction to our conveniences, stop us from growing in spiritual and social matters, seize the American evolution, and bring American ideology into a halt.

We have had periods of time when as a nation we have done greatly and other times when we have suffered from divisions that caused many social and financial hardships among the people. One of the times when, despite suffering all the hardships of a devastating war, our country did well was during World War II. The reason we did well during World War II and after was because America was encouraged to bring in their inventions and creativity. That meant less central government control, more demands for physically and mentally creative jobs and less government spending. This resulted in less control from the IRS and more local government funding to utilize new ideas.

On the other hand, we are going through a period in our history when we will face many future social divisions and internal opposition that will bring our nation into a financial devastation. Large corporations seem to have taken control of our government, local legislatures and their elections, and our daily social and moral lives. We have allowed them to distract us and shift our focus in a destructive direction. We must take simple steps to change our focus and resume the wheel of our economical and ideological existence.

Our first step of correction is to fix the wheel of our economy, making corrections to the misplacement the Realtor movement caused. We also have to find ways to place many jobs in that wheel by creating ecological and reusable resources and new ways to produce energy. Solar, wind, ocean, osmosis, rerouting water, trapping rainwater, all bring jobs that require hiring of large number of engineers, technicians, teachers, research scientists, etc.

This is a focus that actually creates a better-developed society, unites people for a common cause, and increases our integrity in what we do for each other. Real estate, on the other hand, lacks all the characteristics mentioned above, and only drives its vehicle forward by the force of greed. A healthy society based on integrity turns into a group of vulture-like creatures ready to pull the carpet out from underneath one another when there is an opportunity.

What is happening is that the banks have given many easy and unsupported loans to people to buy real estate and houses. Loans were not actually given based on qualifications but only on stated income statements. What could be more deceiving than that? They gave people who could not afford a particular house false hope, raised their expectations, got them into houses, and then, when they default on their loans, the banks take the houses away, along with all the money people invested in those houses as down payment. The banks are robbing people out of their savings. And the irony is that, despite what the banks anticipate, they themselves will be suffering in the long run as a result.

Real estate should be redesigned so that the first-time buyers are able to buy very easily what they can afford, and possibly buy a second property for each member of the family. It should be very hard to buy other real estate that would be considered as investment property unless the properties are in non-metropolitan, non-established, undeveloped, or run-down areas.

In a true capitalistic and minarchy-libertarian society, if your job is a "service" to the public, there should be no taxation of your income in return for your service. Your "service" is what you have already done for the public and the environment, and have been paid for. It is a fair trade.

Taxation must not be allowed for the part of society that is already paying its dues by giving a service to its members. Taxation, however, is allowed and must be done in much greater rates for such productions as entertainment and sports members, movie crew, comedians, TV or show business stars, Wall Street brokers and investors, lottery winners, churches of all kind, and any other income that does not involve a true essential "service" for the public good. Also, in a healthy economical structure, any industry extracting natural resources, (including pharmaceutical companies), insurance companies, and welfare beneficiaries, or recipients of government grants must be subject to taxation.

Our system requires having this great correction so the economical wheels can return to position. Taxation is a requirement to fund and feed the force that turns the wheels of this great system forward. However, this funding and its source of energy must not come as a burden to the "mom and pop" small businesses that build the backbone of our ideological society of America. The IRS must implement this change as soon as possible. If such change does not take place, the IRS, either unintentionally or purposefully, would be the force pulling us toward tyranny. At that point, such an organization would be transformed into a central government force that would continue its authoritarian position by terrorizing the members of the American

Ideology when and if they question the system backed by the tyranny of the majority.

I hope you will give this some thought, and perhaps then together, we can make a change via the world of media, through our daily lives, and within our country. First, let us start the change within the world of media itself, and the corruption it has been infected by, which continuously derails our path of thinking on daily basis. A necessary change is to stop this machine from putting out the very addicting acts of gossip and rumor. The act of gossip and rumors is a destructive illness that disables us as an evolving society. It distracts us from observing the main issues we must pay attention to. We have to stop feeding this disease within such ill machine, and polish and repair it, and instead, utilize it as an educational tool. We have to bring the monster we created ourselves into a halt before it brings us to destruction.

This is an old but very familiar monster that has made a cozy nest within our hearts: The monster we know as the machine of social dogmas and celebrities. The machine that tells us what is right and what is wrong, what looks good and what doesn't, what we may do as a member and what happens to us in shame and torture if we disobey. A machine that can only continue to run if we give it power to do so. Please don't follow. We as individuals truly may know what is right and what may be wrong for us. We can figure it out, and we can decide how to correct this broken wheel, our society on our own if we are dedicated enough to come together and elect the appropriate leaders for this task. In my next series of books, I will start a step-by-step proposition to find ways to place the suitable authorities in required positions.

Authorities are the ones who are responsible to do the jobs that bring unified benefits to all the members of a society. Having authority does not give anyone any power to do whatever they want to. A universal authority is one that would bring unity to all in the existence. And although that may be only possible in a place where there are no borders, no flags, no religions, and, most importantly, no heaven or hell, we have to maintain our borders tight for the time being until we repair the damages from within. The queen and the pope, England and Germany, have taken over our system, our lives, and our freedom, and have enslaved us for their own benefits. They have succeeded in dividing us for the time being. My friends, it is time now to take our system, our lives and our freedom back into our own hands and continue the interrupted journey of human evolution our founding fathers had started in this corner of the world. It is time to step up to the plate and fight back, and take back our liberty, which was stolen away. Kick out the queen and kick out the pope.

I will finish this book with the most important intent we have to focus on in our society. Global terrorism may be an old illness that is poking its infectious head through our Western societies. However, it is our reactions, actions, and proactive thinking which determine what type of affect this illness is going to have on our societies. Our response to a state of emergency will lay ahead the steps we will take into our future, the future of our children along all other species. Universal existence is the state of being in concurrence with everything else, and can only be maintained in the presence of freedom. Free yourself. Free your mind. And let's build a future that will bring a new and better direction to the lives of future human generations in harmony and with respect to all living beings.